Handbook of
Regular Patterns

Handbook of Regular Patterns

An Introduction to
Symmetry in
Two Dimensions

Peter S. Stevens

The MIT Press
Cambridge, Massachusetts,
and London, England

Second printing, 1981

© 1981 by Peter S. Stevens

This book was set in VIP Helvetica by Achorn Graphic Services, Inc. and printed and bound by Halliday Lithograph in the United States of America.

Library of Congress Cataloging in Publication Data

Stevens, Peter S
  Handbook of regular patterns.

  Bibliography: p.
  Includes index.
  1. Repetitive patterns (Decorative arts) 2. Symmetry (Art) 3. Design. I. Title.
NC745.S73
1981   745.4   80-24152
ISBN 0-262-19188-1

*To the unsung artists whose work
we so blithely enjoy, whose work is
so freely borrowed here, whose
work so persistently illuminates
the structure behind appearance*

**IV
The Seventeen
Plane Groups**

Preface

A reading of George Birkhoff's *Aesthetic Measure* provided the inspiration for this work. Birkhoff's concerns for order and complexity in art led him to study different species of repetitive ornament including the seven band groups and the seventeen wallpaper groups. He provided two illustrations for each of those groups. Only two. I carefully studied his illustrations with the hope that I could generate variations of my own. I had only moderate success, however, and not until I reviewed the works of Weyl, Toth, and Buerger was I able to generate patterns easily. Even then I found it difficult to duplicate and imitate the more complex—and more interesting—designs in Owen Jones's *Grammar of Ornament*.

On the one hand there appeared to be an elegant mathematical system of pattern classification used by chemists and crystallographers, and on the other a wealth of repetitive designs in source books used by artists and graphic designers. Birkhoff and Weyl were comfortable in both worlds. After all, crystal sections and wallpaper designs obey the same structural rules—testimony to the harmony that underlies natural and man-made forms. Still, crystallographers and chemists have generally shown limited interest in the source books of artists, and artists know little of the underlying structural anatomy of repetitive groups.

This work attempts a synthesis of the two perspectives. It is an encyclopedia, a reference handbook, of repetitive designs organized in accord with established crystallographic notions of symmetry and symmetry operations.

On the crystallographic side I have adhered to the widely accepted system of classification and notation used in Henry and Lonsdale's *International Tables for X-Ray Crystallography*. For the band ornaments I have adopted a readily understood variation on that notation including the use of the symbols *tm* and *mt* as suggested by Martin Buerger, from whom I also borrowed the idea of using patterns of commas to picture the groups.

Despite its crystallographic backbone, however, the book is directed primarily to the practicing artist and designer. After an initial reading, and perhaps a few practice exercises, the graphic artist can use the chapter headings, running heads, and charts to locate any given structural arrangement. As a practical aid to design, the book provides extensive discussions of unit cells, fundamental regions, centered hexagons, and other generating units. In addition the appendix offers some of the mathematics that underlies repetitive structure. This volume, then, should enable the artist to produce original designs while having at his fingertips numerous examples of structurally similar designs from different cultures and historical periods.

The illustrative examples include designs from nature and architecture as well as ornamental patterns whose origins range from the first and second milleniums before Christ to the twentieth century. Several works are included of the late Dutch artist M. C. Escher, whose technique and use of color symmetry have been analyzed by Caroline Macgillavry in *Fantasy & Symmetry.* I have provided discussions of Escher's design symmetries in order to assist the reader in discovering how to generate additional Escher-like designs. For illustrative purposes I have also included several original designs, especially in the last chapter, which provides a visual recapitulation of the book.

I am especially indebted to the M. C. Escher Foundation, Haags Gemeentemuseum, The Hague, Netherlands, for permission to reproduce the designs of M. C. Escher. I wish also to acknowledge the free use of many designs found in the Dover Pictorial Archive Series. Some of the books that make up that series can be found among the references.

Mollie Moran drafted most of the illustrations and I am deeply indebted to her. I would also like to thank Didi Stevens for her editorial review and Arthur Loeb for his reading of the manuscript and most helpful suggestions.

I
Symmetry Groups

See how various the forms and
how unvarying the principles.

Owen Jones

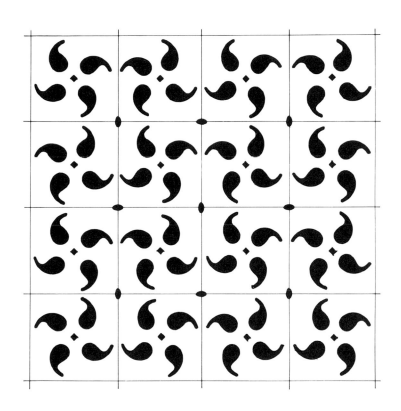

Here and elsewhere we shall not obtain the best insight into things until we actually see them growing from the beginning.

Aristotle

1
Basic Operations

The variety of ornamental pattern is extraordinary. All around us are patterns in textile designs, tiled floors, wallpapers, friezes, and carpets. Animal motifs and foliage patterns abound, but more numerous still are repetitions of abstract forms—circles, crescents, rectangles, and arrangements of stripes and lines. In the natural world too you find repetitive patterns—in the arms of the starfish, in a spiral galaxy, and in the arrangement of leaves on the branches of a tree. Every culture and historical period has produced unique forms and today's designers are busy turning out more.

Symmetry Groups
Mathematicians concerned with the theory of groups hold an interesting view of that variety. They ignore particularities and consider the ways that a motif repeats, the manner in which one part of a pattern relates to the others. The possibilities turn out to be strictly limited. Patterns that run in one direction, linear band ornaments, like those on the borders of wallpaper or the edges of crockery, come in only seven basic types—irrespective of whether the motifs are stylized scorpions along the edge of a Persian rug or leaves of honeysuckle on a Greek vase. Fur-

thermore, you can make only seventeen two-dimensional patterns, patterns that cover a surface—like ceramic mosaics, tiled floors, and arrangements of brickwork.

It was in 1935 that von Franz Steiger proved that only seventeen two-dimensional patterns exist. Unfortunately, Steiger's proof [8: pp. 235–249] makes use of abstract topological concepts that are not particularly useful to designers of patterns. A more useful approach is to catalog patterns in terms of their symmetries. Although repetitive designs have arbitrary features—after all, they may consist of clusters of triangles, birds, or flowers—their symmetries are fixed. Symmetries describe the ways that the arbitrary motifs can be manipulated.

Common Structures
Figures 1 and 2 illustrate the way in which the same structure can underlie different designs. Figure **1.1** shows part of a band of stylized leaves from a Persian ornament of the fifteenth century. This band illustrates one of the seven linear symmetry groups. Notice that the lightly shaded leaves that point up have precisely the same shape as the

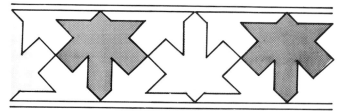

1.1

1.2a

1.2b

heavily shaded ones that point down. Consequently, if you turn the whole band upside-down, it has exactly the same appearance except that the colors reverse. Either way, the outlines of the leaves are precisely the same. Furthermore, each leaf is symmetrical in that its right-hand side is the mirror image of its left-hand side. Assuming that the band extends indefinitely to the right and to the left, you can see that the design as a whole is symmetrical. At the center of any leaf, the right-hand side of the entire band is the mirror image of the left-hand side. Later we will study rotations and mirror reflections in more detail and establish a precise meaning for the term symmetry group, but for now let us observe simply that the band ornament of figure 1 has the same appearance whether upright or upside-down and that the left-hand side is the mirror image of the right-hand side.

Can we find other examples of the same structure? Consider the band ornaments in figure **1.2**. Frame (a) shows a band from Brazil dating from the fourth or fifth century; frame (b), a strap ornament from Elizabethan England; frame (c), an ornamental frieze from ancient Greece; and frame (d), a contemporary design from the United States. Although these ornaments differ from the Persian ornament of figure 1.1, they have exactly the same underlying structure. Each band looks the same whether upright or upside-down, and each band can be divided so that one half is the mirror image of the other half. Whether Persian, Brazilian, English, Greek, or from the United States, whether abstract or floral, whether ancient or modern, all these designs follow the same plan; all have the same anatomy; all belong to the same species of ornament or symmetry group.

Knowledge of symmetry groups can be a great aid to designers. Suppose, for example, that you manufacture patterned concrete blocks. What varieties of design can you offer your customers? How many different walls with repeating patterns can you make from different arrangements of a single motif? If you arrange the blocks in accord with the rules, you can quickly obtain the answers. You will find that any asymmetrical motif can be stacked with itself to create seven linear bands and seventeen planar patterns.

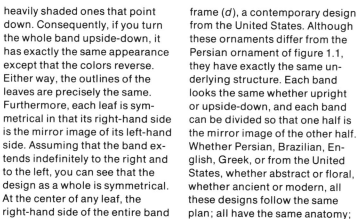

1.2c

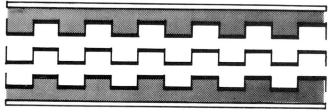

1.2d

Four Symmetry Operations
You will gain a good start toward understanding the structure of regular patterns when you realize that a two-dimensional motif can repeat in only four different ways. These four types of repetition, or symmetry operations as they are called, are worth studying because combinations of them produce all of the different symmetry groups. The four operations are (1) translation, in which the motif moves up or down, left or right, or diagonally while keeping the same orientation; (2) rotation, in which the motif turns; (3) reflection, in which the motif reflects as in a mirror; and (4) glide reflection, in which the motif both translates and reflects.

Repetition of the asymmetric comma shown in figure **1.3** illustrates these four operations in an elegant fashion. For the ancient Persians the comma—the familiar paisley pattern as well as our

1.3

common punctuation mark—was a venerated motif. Some scholars consider the mark a stylized flame and trace its history through Zoroastrian cults to the primitive worship of fire. Others prefer the tale that an Iranian artist's young son dipped his hand into his father's pot of paint and imprinted a piece of linen with the side of his half-curled fist.

Translation
The commas in figure **1.4** show three examples of the first symmetry operation, translation. The frames of the figure show the commas translated horizontally, vertically, and diagonally. You can imagine that the Iranian boy stood opposite you as you look at the page and, working with his left hand, kept his wrist stiff as he made his marks. Each comma in a framed pair is a translation of the other. This idea is important because every operation is a two-way street. Every operation shifts the second image into the first image as well as the first image into the second. If you view all three frames as a totality, commas in any pair are each other's translation, irrespective of whether they reside in the same frame.

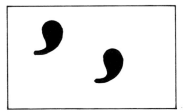

1.4

Rotation

Figure **1.5** illustrates the second symmetry operation with three sets of commas. In these examples the boy turned his fist between the first and second print of each pair. It is important to realize that no translations are involved; only rotations. If you rotate one comma of a pair around the point marked in the frame, you can superimpose it exactly on the other comma. To be certain, redraw one of the commas in the first frame on a piece of tracing paper and, with your pencil, pin the paper to the dot that marks the center of rotation; you can then turn the paper so that the comma you have drawn coincides with the other. Do the same for the commas in the other frames. Now if you consider the three frames together, you find that any comma in any frame is a rotation of any of the others. Try to locate, for example, the center of rotation that relates the lower comma in the top frame to the upper comma in the middle frame. See if you can locate similar centers of rotation for other pairs.

As you study figure 1.5 you will discover that distant centers of rotation, or rotocenters as they are commonly called, produce apparent translations. As a case in point, note the apparent translation between the upper commas in the top and middle frames. Those commas are related by rotation through a distant rotocenter.

Figure **1.6** shows the idea with greater clarity. The dot in the top frame is the center of rotation for all three pairs of commas. Each successive pair, at increasing distance from the rotocenter, shows less twist and more sweep. Consequently we can see that pure translation is but a special case of rotation—rotation through an infinitely small angle or, what amounts to the same thing, rotation around a center that lies infinitely far away.

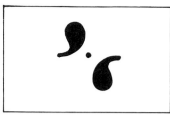

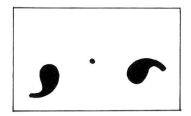

1.5

1.6

By way of review, see if you can identify the relation of each unshaded comma in figure **1.10** to the shaded one in the center. You should find two glide reflections and one translation, rotation, and mirror reflection. Which operations are direct? Which indirect?

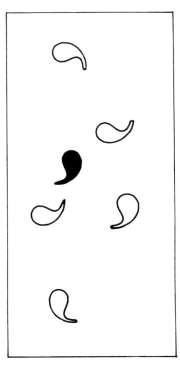

1.10

Exercises

1. What operations describe the relation between the two triangles in each frame of figure **1.11**? What special characteristic of the triangles in the last frame leads you to name two different operations?

2. Sprinkle cardboard cutouts of an asymmetric motif on a surface and describe the relations among them. How are those that flip over related to those that do not?

3. In figure **1.12**, reflect the comma in mirror line a. Then reflect the resulting image in line b. How does the final image relate to the original comma? Relative to the distance between mirror lines, how far is the final image from the original? Would the results be the same for every motif reflected in parallel mirrors?

4. In figure **1.13**, reflect the comma in mirror line a. Then reflect the resulting image in mirror line b. How is the final image related to the original comma? If the angle between the two lines is 45°, what is the angle between the final image and the original? What would be the angle between the final and original image if the angle between the lines was 90°?

5. In each frame of Figure **1.14**, reflect the comma in mirror line a, the resulting image in line b, and that next image in line c. In each frame, how does the final image relate to the original comma? (Don't worry about overlapping images.)

6. Show that a translation results from successive reflections in two parallel mirrors, a rotation results from reflection in two mirrors that intersect, and a glide reflection results from successive reflections in two parallel and one perpendicular mirror. (This exercise should provide a check for the others.)

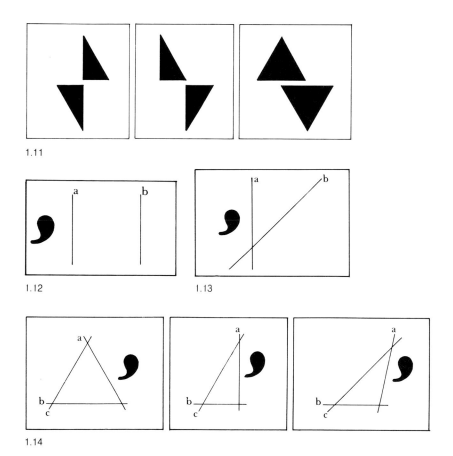

1.11

1.12

1.13

1.14

2
How Operations Generate Themselves

With the aid of displacements and reversals of commas, we have examined the four symmetry operations that produce repetition. We are now in a position to tackle the meaning of symmetry.

Symmetry

If the comma is an asymmetric figure, what is a symmetric one? The answer is that a symmetric figure has repetitive parts. And how might the parts of a figure repeat? Just as we have discovered: by translation, rotation, reflection, and glide reflection.

Letters A, B, and C, for instance, are symmetrical through reflection. They enjoy bilateral symmetry in which one half is the mirror image of the other. A mirror through the center of these letters leaves their appearance unaltered. And this is the critical point. A figure is symmetrical if a symmetry operation such as a mirror reflection leaves its appearance unchanged.

Letters N and Z are symmetrical by virtue of rotation. A 180°-turn leaves their appearance unchanged because one half of the letter is exactly like the other. You may find the symmetry of N and Z surprising since we commonly use the word symmetrical to mean bilaterally symmetrical. We would all agree, for example, that the letter A is symmetrical. Although the letters N and Z are not symmetrical in the manner of A, they are also symmetrical since their parts repeat by rotation. Similarly, the word "bud" is symmetrical because of mirror reflection, the word "pod" is symmetrical under rotation, and the word "dodo" is symmetrical by virtue of translation.

Symmetry Groups

We are closing in on the definition of the term symmetry group.

Consider the pattern in figure **2.1**. The center is marked with a small diamond, which is the conventional indication of a fourfold rotation. You can see that four operations (rotations) displace the pattern to four equivalent positions: (1) rotation through a quarter-turn or 90°; (2) through a half-turn or 180°; (3) through a three-quarter turn or 270°; and (4) through a full turn or 360°, back to the original position.

Figure **2.2** portrays another pattern with the same symmetry. It is important to realize that although each arm of figure 2.2 contains two commas related by a mirror, the individual mirrors do not reflect the entire pattern into

2.1

2.2

equivalent positions. The pattern then—as a whole—has only fourfold rotational symmetry. Consequently, figures 2.1 and 2.2 belong to the same symmetry group.

A Definition
Now then, the definition of the term symmetry group. A symmetry group is a collection of symmetry operations that together share three characteristics: (1) each operation can be followed by a second operation to produce a third operation that itself is a member of the group, (2) each operation can be undone by another operation, that is to say, for each operation there exists an inverse operation, and (3) the position of the pattern after an operation can be the same as before the operation, that is, there exists an identity operation which leaves the figure unchanged.

You can see that the definition is very abstract. Perhaps though, you can see how the operations that rotate figures 2.1 and 2.2 form a symmetry group. Here is an enumeration that accords with the definition. (1) The 90° rotation can be followed by a 180° rotation to produce a 270° rotation which itself is a member of the group. (2) A 90° rotation can be undone

by a 90° rotation in the opposite direction. Any of the other rotations can similarly be followed by inverse rotations. (3) A full turn of 360° brings the pattern back to where it began. Any rotation that is a multiple of 360° also leaves the pattern in the same position.

Generating Groups
Where do we go from here? At this point we can see how the operations feed upon themselves to produce still larger groups. As an example, let us add another operation to the fourfold center. Let us pass a mirror directly through its heart and study the results step-by-step.

Figure **2.3a** shows a mirror through a fourfold center, with each of the four arms identified. As indicated in figure 2.3b, arms a, b, c, and d reflect to produce arms a', b', c', and d'. The result of all those reflections appears in figure 2.3c. Now you find that the pattern contains four intersecting mirrors. A single mirror through a fourfold rotocenter produces automatically four intersecting mirrors.

All the reflections and the rotations together form a symmetry group because they obey the following conditions: they produce

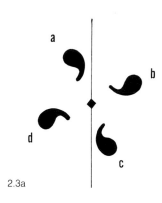

2.3a

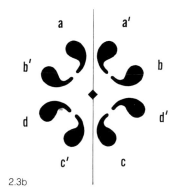

2.3b

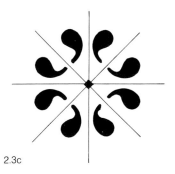

2.3c

2.4a

additional reflections and rotations, they can be undone by inverse operations, and some combinations of them leave the position of the pattern unchanged. The entire symmetry group contains eight operations: four reflections and four rotations. All these operations leave the appearance of the pattern unaltered.

As another illustration of the manner in which symmetry groups come into being, consider placing the mirror line next to a fourfold design instead of through its heart. The arrangement is depicted in figure **2.4a**.

Taking the results step-by-step, you find that the mirror reflects the rotating pattern to produce the double image shown in figure 2.4b. You can see how the two rotocenters interrelate like a pair of oppositely rotating paddle wheels. But this is only part of the story, for if the original rotocenter continues to rotate, it shifts the mirror along with the reflected image into the four positions shown in Figure 2.4c. It thus produces four mirrors. At this point,

2.4b

the action continues because each mirror reflects and each rotocenter rotates, and all together they generate, in the twinkling of the eye, an endless array of images in all directions across the plane. A portion of the infinite pattern appears in figure **2.5.**

What are the operations in figure 2.5?

First there are fourfold rotocenters like the motif of figure 2.1, except that in the infinite pattern the whole pattern rotates. In other words, the rotating motif consists now of more than four commas; it includes the whole two-dimensional plane with all the fourfold centers and all the mirror lines. To verify that the entire pattern repeats with each 90° rotation, draw the pattern on tracing paper and rotate it around each rotocenter. You will see the entire pattern repeat again and again. In addition to clockwise rotations you find mirror-image counterclockwise rotations. Both types of rotocenter act on the entire plane.

Next you find that the infinite pattern has generated two different sets of parallel mirror lines that intersect perpendicularly. Every mirror reflects the entire infinite pattern into itself.

2.4c

2.5

Last, you discover twofold rotocenters that lie on each intersection of the mirror lines. In accord with convention they are marked with an oval. Figure **2.6** shows a small portion of the twofold center in its two different orientations. Each twofold center contains the same symmetry operations as the letter H: a vertical reflection, a horizontal reflection, and a 180° rotation.

As with the mirrors and the fourfold rotations, remember that each twofold center acts not only on the eight commas shown in figure 2.6 but on all the commas in the infinite pattern. In other words the entire pattern forms a twofold rotocenter. Even more to the point, the entire pattern forms an infinite number of twofold rotocenters. Some have the orientation shown in figure 2.6a, the others have the orientation shown in figure 2.6b. In addition, as already described, the pattern forms an infinite number of left-handed and right-handed four-fold centers—plus an infinite number of perpendicularly intersecting mirror lines. All these elements are interrelated and perfectly spaced to repeat and regenerate endlessly. All this interactive creation and re-creation flashes into existence when a fourfold rotation mates with a mirror line.

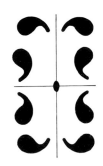

2.6a

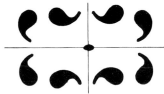

2.6b

Figure 2.5, then, illustrates one of the seventeen two-dimensional plane groups. It is a uniquely interactive association of symmetry operations. Of course, the repetitive element could be the letter P, a flower, or a bird, as well as a comma. The invariant elements are the structural operations.

A Further Example

For comparison, let us look at another example of the same symmetry group. Figure **2.7** shows (a) a fourfold center, (b) the same center reflected once, and (c) the same center reflected four times. Further rotations and reflections produce the design of figure **2.8** which, when colored, results in the leaf pattern of figure **2.9.**

This pattern occurred as a painted decoration in a house in Cairo in the fifteenth century. It consists of only a single motif expressed in three different colors. A linear band of the pattern was depicted in figure 1.1

The interesting point is that the leaf form in figure 2.9 performs exactly the same maneuvers as the comma in figure 2.5—clockwise and counterclockwise fourfold rotations, mirror reflections, and twofold rotations. Figures 2.5 and 2.9 express exactly the same thought, but in different languages.

2.7a

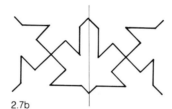

2.7b

2.7c

You can now sense why there exists a limited number of symmetry groups: the rotations rotate the reflections and all the other rotations, and the reflections reflect each other and all the rotations combined. All the operations must interact with themselves to produce more of the same sort of interaction. Each symmetry group, then, is a closed system of self-generating operations where all operations are interrelated.

The Dutch artist, M. C. Escher, who created a wealth of novel designs, grasped the beauty and lawfulness of these self-generating operations:

There is something in such laws that takes the breath away. They are not discoveries or inventions of the human mind, but exist independently of us. In a moment of clarity, one can at most discover that they are there and take them into account. [52: p. 40]

2.8

2.9

Exercises

1. What symmetry operation leaves the appearance of the comma in figure 1.3 unchanged?

2. What two symmetry operations make up the symmetry group described by the commas in the first frame of figure 1.4?

3. How many symmetry operations make up the group described by the commas in the first frame of figure 1.5?

4. What operations leave unchanged the appearance of the letters in figure **2.10**?

5. If instead of adding a mirror to the side of the fourfold rotocenter shown in figure 2.4a, you add it to the side of the rotocenter shown in figure 2.3c, would the resulting infinite pattern contain the same operations as the pattern of figure 2.5? Do you think the two infinite patterns would belong to the same symmetry group?

6. What operations exist in figure **2.11**? Does the pattern belong to the symmetry group displayed in figure 2.5?

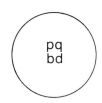

2.10

2.11

II
Point Groups

The whole and each particular member should be a multiple of some simple unit.

Owen Jones

	1	m	2	2mm	3	3m	4	4mm	6	6mm
No Reflections	t		t2							
Centers on Mirrors		tm		t2mm						
Mirrors and Glides		mt	t2mg							
Glide Reflections	tg									

Point Groups

1	m	2	2mm	3	3m	4	4mm	6	6mm
1	m	2	2mm	3	3m	4	4mm	6	6mm

	1	m	2	2mm	3	3m	4	4mm	6	6mm
No Reflections	p1		p2		p3		p4		p6	
Centers on Mirrors		pm		p2mm		p3m1		p4mm		p6mm
Mirrors and Glides	cm		p2mg	c2mm		p31m	p4gm			
Glide Reflections	pg		p2gg							

3.1

3
Point Groups

Two-dimensional symmetry groups fall into three general classes. The first class, which we will study in this section, consists of point groups, in which the motif rotates about a fixed point. The fourfold rotocenter in figure 1.12 exemplifies the category. The second class consists of patterns that stretch in a line, and the third class encompasses repetitive patterns that spread uniformly across the plane. We will study the latter categories, the line and plane groups, in the next two sections.

Leonardo da Vinci first catalogued the point groups. He designed churches that incorporated radiating chapels arranged around a central point like the petals of a flower. An example appears in figure **3.2.** If you ignore the entrance, you can see how the plan of the church represents a symmetry group, for under rotations and reflections it maintains the same appearance.

Point Groups in Nature
Flowers, starfish, sea urchins, jelly fish, and sea anemones display that same type of rotational or radial symmetry. How does that symmetry arise? Why are some creatures symmetrical and others asymmetrical?

Small water-borne animals like the diatoms shown in figure **3.3** have spherical symmetry. Owing to their small size, they bob and spin in the waves oblivious to gravity, unconcerned with the directions of up, down, and sideways. They drift freely in a uniform environment and consequently have no need for differentiated bodies, for ends, sides, tops, and bottoms.

Living forms that attach to a surface or move slowly across the ground distinguish up and down. They may have stems like flowers and hydra or they may have primitive feet like starfish. Figure **3.4** shows a sea anemone attached by a suckered foot to the glass wall of an aquarium. Those sessile creatures develop a top and a bottom, but have no sense of forward, backward, or right and left. Because these directions are interchangeable, the creatures put forth identical appendages in all directions; they develop radial symmetry.

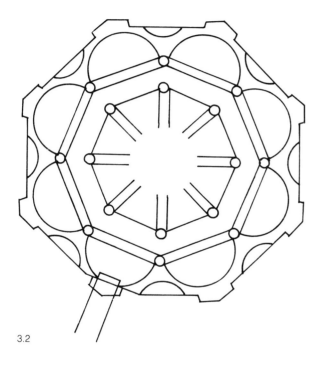

3.2

3.3

3.4

Most animals, however, have bilateral symmetry. Like radial forms, they have a top and bottom, a back and a belly, but in addition they have a head and a tail. Why? Because they move actively about. With active movement, their radially distributed appendages differentiate so that a head develops to lead the way, lateral appendages provide balanced propulsion from the sides, and a tail brings up the rear.

You can imagine that if the environment on one side of a bilateral creature differs from the environment on the other, the creature might develop a completely asymmetric form. You may have heard the joke about grazing sheep that always circle a hill in the same direction so that their legs on the downhill side grow longer than those on the uphill side. To catch them you need only approach from the front, so that, when they turn to run away, they roll down the hill.

In reality, of course, no asymmetric sheep have developed. But consider asymmetric fish. They are just as strange. When the flounder swam in an upright position, the environment on its right

was like that on its left and it developed bilateral symmetry. When the fish changed its habits to swim on its side, however, the mud of the bottom was of less interest than the clear water above and the eye that faced the mud migrated into a position alongside the other eye to gaze upward. The result is a startling asymmetry in flounders in which both eyes peer from the same side of an otherwise symmetric body.

The conclusion is clear. Whereas a uniform environment produces a living form with a high degree of symmetry, a differentiated environment produces a differentiated or asymmetric form.

Discrete Amounts

The starfish exhibits a still more general trait. It has five arms, or, depending on its species, nine, twelve, or some other specific number of arms. Except for an injured individual, you do not find starfish with 4½ arms or 3.14159. . . arms.

Many things come in discrete or integral amounts—like the fingers on your hand or the number of electrons in an atom. But many other things do not. You do not have to fill a glass with exactly two or exactly three fingers of Scotch. You can use your discretion. Furthermore, that Scotch does not have to contain a specific number of atoms to taste like Scotch.

Nature draws a sharp line between things that come in discrete amounts and things that come in arbitrary amounts. The symmetry operations epitomize discreteness. They either combine precisely to make symmetry groups, or they do not. In point

groups, for example, each rotation must unite with other rotations to make a full turn. In more complex groups each reflection must reflect rotated elements which are themselves reflected and rotated. In order to make a symmetry group, all the maneuvers must interlock with discrete and exacting precision.

Do you sense the equilibrium and harmony in the symbols of figure **4.3**? Does their familiarity make them only seem correct, or has each one been carefully tailored over the years to swoop and curve with pleasing grace?

Through obvious repetition, the Mexican bird motifs of figure **4.4** show a conscious attempt to achieve balance. In the Walpi bird (American Indian) of figure **4.5** the similar treatment of the tail and head reinforces the almost perfect line of reflection through the doubled feathers of the back.

4.3a

4.3b

4.3c

4.4a

4.4b

4.4c

4.5

Figure **4.6** shows more Mexican images, while figure **4.7** shows a piece of wall tile from the medieval period and the motif of a lightning bolt from a Japanese family crest. Each design wraps around itself with a regularity that belies its basic asymmetry.

Although the patterns in figures 4.1 through 4.7 are asymmetric, they achieve balance through subtle repetitions of their parts and the establishment of well-placed centers of interest. Whether in painting, weaving, sculpture, or architecture, nearly every artist adopts these strategies; he makes one part echo another around developed centers of attention.

Most symmetry groups produce repetitions and centers of interest more directly. In symmetry groups each repetition precisely duplicates the others, and the centers are rotocenters around which the entire pattern revolves.

4.6a

4.6b

4.6c

4.7a

4.7b

You might suppose that asymmetric creations have a more subtle execution than symmetric ones. You might suppose that an imitation and a general focus of interest will arouse more aesthetic pleasure than an exact duplication and a defined rotocenter. But not always. Repetitive patterns achieve variety and interest through the immensely complicated interrelations of their parts. One part of the pattern transposes or reflects another part while also repeating a third part in a still different fashion. And yet, all the parts fit inevitably together in an endless fabric of interdependent operations. In few other realms will you find such an arresting combination of surprise and inevitability.

5
Bilateral Symmetry:
Group *m*

The addition of a mirror to an asymmetric motif produces a pattern with bilateral symmetry. We have seen examples of bilateral symmetry in figure 1.7 which shows reflections of commas. Mirror reflection is a member of the family of point groups because, like the asymmetric motif of group 1, a full rotation about a central point brings the pattern into coincidence with itself. We will designate this mirror group by the small letter *m*.

Designations

At this point, a general statement regarding the designations of groups may be useful. A bewildering variety of designations exists because different authors have emphasized different aspects of the groups. We have already seen that groups have multifaceted personalities and that each element in a pattern may be a product of several different operations.

Two systems of description enjoy current popularity, the Hermann-Mauguin system used by crystallographers and the Schoenflies system used by spectroscopists and chemists. It is generally conceded that the Hermann-Mauguin system is more concise. Wherever possible, then, it is the system used in this book. The only exception is for the line groups, which are not usually included in crystallographic descriptions. For the line groups, however, we will use designations that are compatible with the Hermann-Mauguin system.

Bilateral Symmetry

Now, back to bilateral symmetry. We have learned that creatures that move actively about develop a symmetric body—a head and a tail with symmetrically distributed lateral appendages. As examples, figure **5.1** shows renderings of (a) a lizard from Mexico, (b) a lizard from Mali in West Africa, (c) a dragonfly from the northwestern United States, (d) a bear from the northwestern United States, and (e) a painted hide produced by the Haida Indians of British Columbia.

5.1a

5.1b

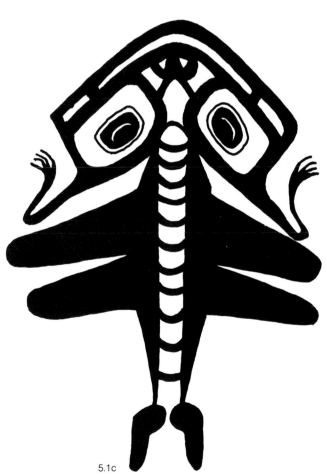

5.1c

5.1d

5.1e

As illustrated in figures **5.2** and **5.3,** the human figure also follows a bilateral plan. Figure 5.2 is from Agrippa. Figure 5.3 shows (a) a design from the Italian Renaissance, (b) a Hopi Indian motif, (c) a design from Panama, and (d) a pattern produced by the Inca Indians of pre-Columbian Peru.

Of course, the actual view of a human being is seldom face-to-face in a manner that produces appreciation of bilateral symmetry. You usually view a person obliquely, as he moves about, not as he would appear if spread-eagled on a dissecting table. The symmetric expressions of animal and human forms in figures 5.1–5.3 are structural diagrams rather than natural views. They portray the plan or design of the creature rather than its appearance.

In addition the symmetry of a body seldom holds in every detail. We are all a little crooked. Our stomachs turn and our hearts are in the wrong place. We have cowlicks, and unique fingerprints on each finger. Whereas the palm of one hand is said to reveal the self with which we were born, the palm of the other supposedly depicts the self we can become.

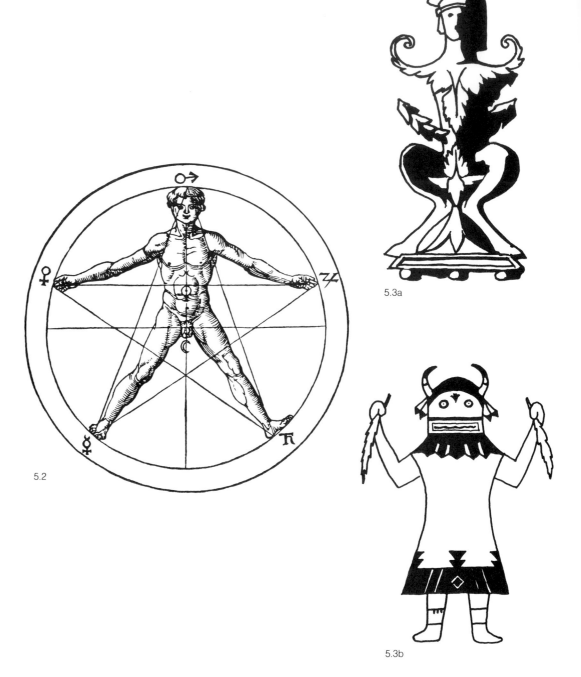

5.2

5.3a

5.3b

5.3c

5.3d

If you look into a mirror with someone you know very well, you will find that the other person's face looks twisted and distorted, but each of you will think your own face looks fine. You are familiar with the asymmetric idiosyncrasies of your own mirror image but not with the reflected image of another person. Perhaps this is why many people find photographs of themselves unnatural. With respect to their familiar mirror image, the photograph switches left and right. Narcissus too fell in love with his mirrored rather than his real self.

Figure **5.4** carries the bilateral image one step further. Apparently, many artists have found two heads or two bodies better than one. The double-headed eagle in frame (a) is from the Romanesque period; the one in (b) is from ancient Mexico. According to Hermann Weyl, the image of the double-headed eagle originated in ancient Sumaria and passed to Persia, Syria, and then Byzantium. It served in the coat-of-arms of the Austro-Hungarian monarchy and Czarist Russia. Today it exists on the Albanian flag.

The fish with two bodies is a Mimbres pottery design (American Indian), and the two-headed snake is a Mixtec ornament from Mexico.

In the examples of the eagles and the fish you could say that the artist has portrayed the two side views of the same head or body rather than a creature with two different heads or bodies. The Mixtec snake scotches that view, however. The Mixtec snake is obviously a two-headed freak. In that example truth defers to an appearance of order.

5.4a

5.4b

5.4c

5.4d

Beyond Realism

Why does the artistic expression of bilateral symmetry in these illustrations overpower the realistic image? Perhaps the answer is that a mirror reflection contains a winning combination of both dynamic and static expressions. Along the line of the mirror the image has directivity—a head and a tail. But on the sides the image repeats with a comfortable and easily recognizable regularity.

Figure **5.5** shows images created by bodies that touch tangentially rather than fuse, so that the mirror passes outside rather than through their bodies. The cocks in frame (a) are from Pazyryk in Siberia and date from about 400 B.C. The dolphins in (b) are from eighteenth-century Sweden. The birds in (c) may be from China.

In figure **5.6**, which shows a Tlingit design from southeastern Alaska, the mirror pierces the body of the bear so that the disembodied eyes and killer whales with fins that become faces float on each side in perfect balance.

5.5a

5.5b

5.5c

5.6

5.7

Growth and Bilateral Symmetry

Not only animals possess bilateral symmetry. Figure **5.7** shows a doubled branch of mock orange in which pairs of leaves grow along each stem in the "opposite" pattern. Figure **5.8** shows three Greek vase ornaments with the same symmetry.

In architecture, too, growth and movement produce bilateral symmetry. Processional movement is incorporated in the symmetric plan of Amiens cathedral shown in figure **5.9**. The apse, narthex, side chapels, and transept correspond to the head, tail, and balanced appendages of an organic creature. The facade has the same symmetry. Each side mirrors the other around the axis of the entrance. Most architectural elevations follow the same pattern, from Stonehenge to the modern office building.

The bilateral image everywhere abounds, in the trident and the arrow, in the sergeant's stripes and the archbishop's cross, in the human skull and the parabolic trail of a comet. Bilateral symmetry expresses balanced growth along a single axis.

5.8a

5.8b

5.8c

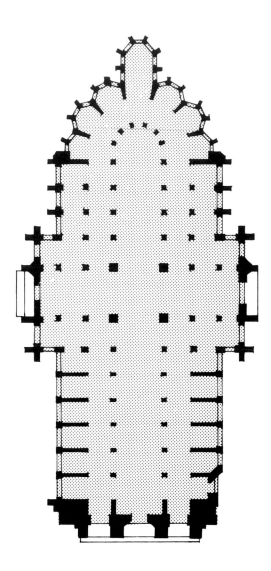

5.9

Exercises

1. What is the group designation of the Celtic manuscript ornaments in figure **5.10**?

2. Why don't the letters of figure 2.10 belong to group *m*?

3. Indicate which of the following letters belong to group 1 and which to group *m*: O,P,E,R,A,T,I,O,N,S. Are you sure about letters I,O,N, and S? Do they contain rotations or additional mirrors?

4. To what point group would you assign duplicate images of the two-headed bird shown in figure 5.4b if the images are separated by a translation? Would the direction of the translation matter?

5. To what point group would you assign duplicate images of the two-headed bird shown in figure 5.4b if the images are related by a 90° rotation? (Draw the resulting figure to be certain.)

5.10a

5.10b

6
Playing Cards
and Walnuts:
Groups 2 and *2mm*

Group 2
The design of a playing card like the Jack-of-Diamonds in figure **6.1** ensures that it will appear the same right-side-up and upside-down, that it will have an identical appearance after a turn through 180°. To accomplish this feat, the designer must use an image with a twofold rotocenter, an image that belongs to group 2.

Patterns of group 2 consist often of two parts that rotate about each other like dogs chasing around a tree. In addition to the pair of commas, the illustrative examples in figure **6.2** show Mimbres Indian designs—lady bugs and birds—and a Japanese design of millipedes from a family crest. In frame (a) notice the oval which is the standard symbol for a twofold rotocenter.

6.1

6.2a

6.2b

6.2d

6.2c

6.3a

In figure **6.3** the double images portray hands, one pair from ancient Mexico, the other from a modern sign that identifies an office for the exchange of currency. Figure **6.4** also juxtaposes the new with the old. The interlocked design of frame (a) comes from ancient Mexico, whereas frame (b) pictures the couplers that link two railroad cars.

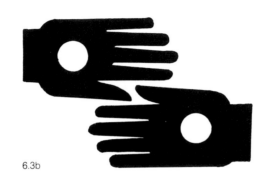

6.3b

6.4a

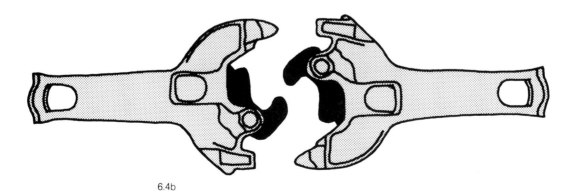

6.4b

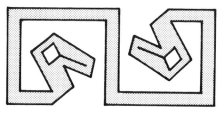

6.5a

Figure **6.5** portrays one- and two-headed snakes twisted and intertwined to appear the same when turned through 180°. Design (a) originated in pre-Columbian Peru, (b) in Michoachan, Mexico, (c) in ancient Mississippi, (d) in China, and (e) in Coatepec, Mexico. Intertwining also characterizes the symbolic knot as well as the sheepshank knot in figure **6.6**.

6.5b

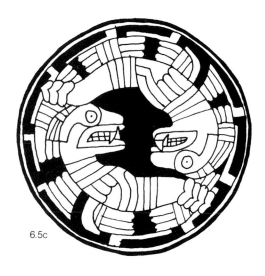

6.5c

6.5d

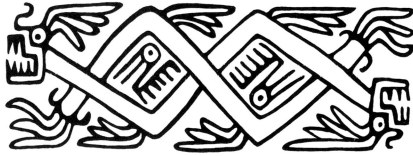

6.5e

6.6a

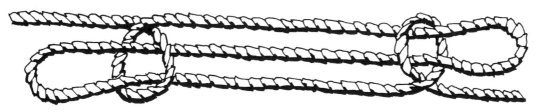

6.6b

We find a natural example of a group-2 pattern in the double-barred spiral galaxy (NGC 1300) of figure **6.7**. Figure **6.8** portrays two ancient symbols belonging to the same group, the runic symbol for death and the well-known Chinese yin-yang symbol of universal duality. You might also consider in figure **6.9** the group-2 optical illusion that so intrigued M. C. Escher.

6.7

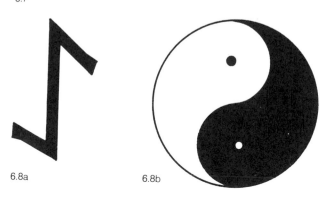

6.8a

6.8b

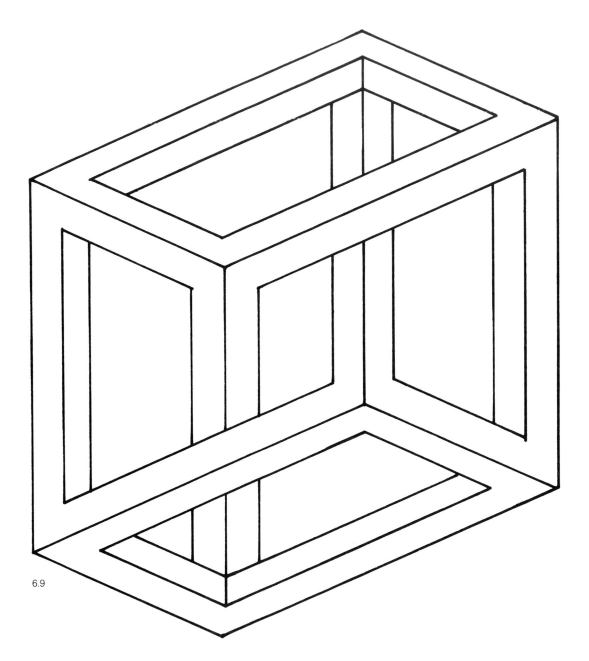

6.9

Group *2mm*

What happens when you pass a mirror through the center of a group-2 pattern? You get automatically the pattern of group *2mm* which contains a twofold center and two perpendicular mirrors.

Figure **6.10** shows a naturally occurring example of the *2mm* pattern in the cross section of a walnut. The section of walnut appears the same when rotated 180°, just as for group-2 patterns; but in addition, the image has bilateral symmetry around both its horizontal and vertical axes.

The two perpendicular mirrors are shown explicitly for the arrangement of commas in figure **6.11**. Can you see how reflecting a simple group-2 image in a single mirror produces additional reflections in the second mirror? We came across a similar example in figure 2.3 when we discovered that a single mirror through a fourfold center produces a pattern of four intersecting mirrors.

6.10

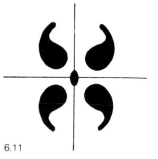

6.11

The Addition of Mirrors

It turns out that a single mirror through any *n*-fold center produces *n* mirrors where *n* can be any integral number. Thus the addition of a mirror through the center of rotation in groups 1, 2, 3, 4, 5, and 6 produces 1, 2, 3, 4, 5, and 6 mirrors. In the Hermann-Mauguin notation the designations for these point groups with mirrors are *m*, 2*mm*, 3*m*, 4*mm*, 5*m*, and 6*mm*. (Group *m* could be written 1*m*, but the 1 is generally omitted. Some authors also omit the 2 from the 2*mm* designation.) The *m* is doubled in groups with an even number of rotations to indicate the presence of two types of mirrors. Those mirrors are discussed later—in the text that accompanies figure 8.8. Groups with an odd number of rotations contain only one type of mirror and are thus designated with a single *m*.

The groups that are produced by adding mirrors to simple rotocenters can also be produced when mirrors are used alone, because, as we saw in exercise 3 at the end of the first chapter, two intersecting mirrors create rotations as well as reflections.

The use of mirrors to generate point groups has a fascinating practical application. If, as pictured in figure **6.12**, you tape two mirrors together along a common edge and stand them on a table, an object placed between them will reflect and re-reflect so that every other reflection is a rotation through twice the angle between the mirrors. Consequently, to obtain patterns 2*mm*, 3*m*, 4*mm*, and 5*m*, the mirrors are set so that the angle between them is 90°, 60°, 45°, and 36°. If you vary the angle between the mirrors, you can see easily how the mirrors reproduce images and you will be in a position to understand better the arrangements of mirrors that generate more complex groups.

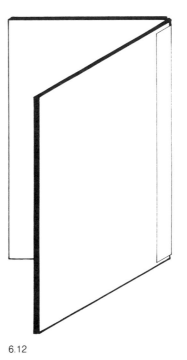

6.12

Figure **6.13** shows 2*mm* images in which each quadrant is clearly separated by implicit mirror lines. The designs are from (a) India, (b) the Yucatan, and (c) ancient Greece. In figure **6.14** the images are fused. Frame (a) shows a Renaissance stone mason's mark, frame (b) the Chinese "gold coin" design of good luck.

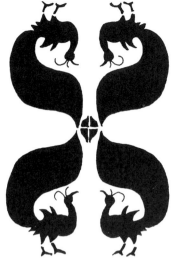

6.13a

6.13b

6.13c

6.14a

6.14b

Culture and Symmetry

See if you can guess the origins of the 2*mm* designs in figure **6.15**. Which come from Ethiopia, Connecticut (early Indian), Siberia, and Czechoslovakia? The answers are (a) Siberia, (b) Czechoslovakia, (c) Connecticut, and (d) Ethiopia. How good were your guesses? Now try to match the designs in figure **6.16** with their origins: pre-Columbian Peru, Turkey, ancient Mexico, Celtic Ireland, and modern Denmark. The order of the origins turns out to be the same as the order in which the designs are presented.

From such guessing games you learn that different cultures produce designs that are much the same. The similarities do not necessarily arise because the cultures copy one another but because the constraints of space decree the existence of a limited number of symmetry groups, and designs within the same group tend to look alike.

6.15a

6.15c

6.15b

6.15d

6.16a

6.16b

6.16c

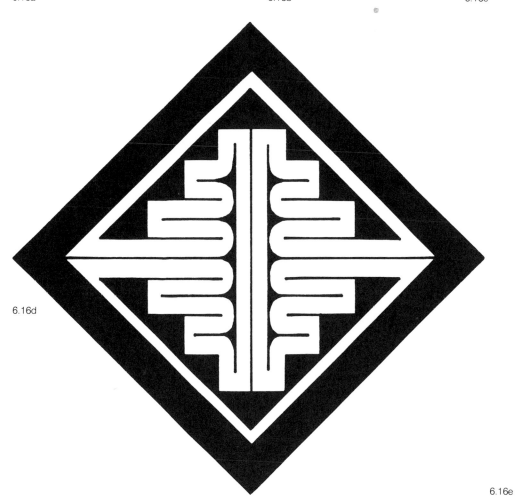

6.16d

6.16e

Exercises

1. In what ways does the drawing by M. C. Escher in figure **6.17**, which shows neither a rotation nor a reflection, contain aspects of both?

2. To what group do the letters of figure 2.10 belong?

3. Indicate which of the following letters belong to groups 1, *m*, 2, and *2mm*: O,P,E,R,A,T,I,O,N,S. Are you sure about the letter O?

4. To what point group would you assign two walnuts like the one in figure 6.10 if they were separated by a translation? Would the direction of the translation matter?

5. If you stand spread-eagled directly in front of a mirror, what group do you and your image generate? (Imagine the view of someone looking straight down on you from above so that you and your reflected image are seen in plan as in an architectural drawing.) If you stand in a similar fashion facing the intersection of two perpendicular mirrors like those you might find in a clothing store, what group do you and your images generate? How many images will you see? How many of those images are capable of making a motion to shake hands with you in the conventional fashion—right hand to right hand?

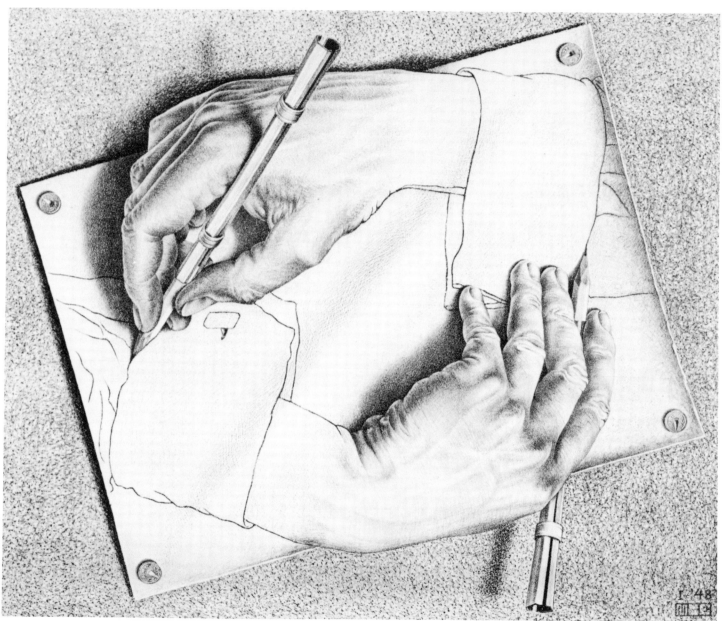

6.17

7
The Triskelion and the Green Pepper: Group 3 and 3*m*

Group 3

Three rotations bring a group-3 pattern into coincidence with itself: a 120° rotation, a 240° rotation, and a 360° rotation. In figure **7.1** the pattern of group 3 is illustrated by commas surrounding the solid triangle, which is the standard symbol for a threefold rotocenter. Frames (b) and (c) show Japanese stylized commas and a Chinese Turkestan motif of a triple flame.

The group-3 pattern is the epitome of vitality and movement. It hums with rotational action. In figure **7.2** we see (a) an abstract triskelion, (b) a fully developed triskelion from ancient Greece, and (c) the framing of a Gothic window. They all appear to rotate on their own accord.

Interlaced group-3 variations have enjoyed great popularity. Frames (a) and (b) in figure **7.3** were symbols for the Holy Trinity long before they became popular as advertizing logos. It is likely that those images developed independently of the Japanese motifs in frames (c) and (d).

7.1a

7.1b

7.2a

7.3a

7.3b

7.1c

7.2b

7.3c

7.2c

7.3d

Snakes have often been depicted in interlaced patterns. Figure **7.4** shows a modern group-3 drawing of snakes by M. C. Escher.

A handsome group-3 symbol in current use is the copyrighted symbol for wool products shown in figure **7.5**a. The symbol for recyclable containers in figure 7.5b looks at first glance as if it too belongs to group 3. To what group does it actually belong? (If you have to, trace and rotate the figure.)

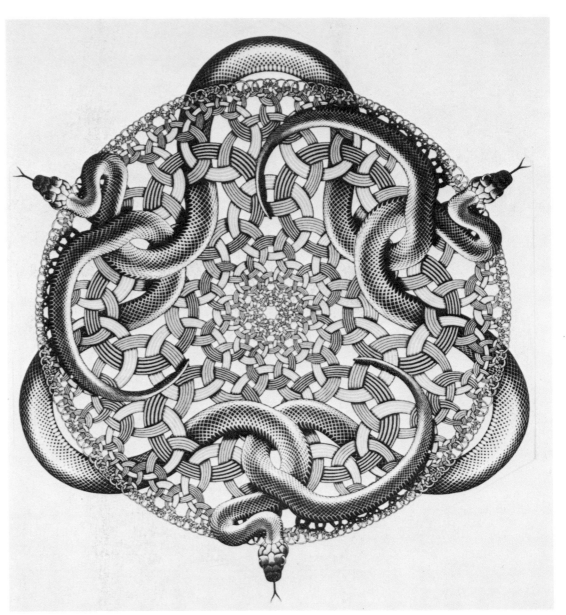

7.4

7.6a

Group 3*m*

Group 3*m* patterns have three bilaterally symmetric arms spaced at 120°. Figure **7.6** shows some interesting examples: (a) six commas; (b) beetles on a Japanese crest; (c) a Mycenaean motif from early Greece; (d) a Nordic rune to induce madness; (e) an architectural plan of a church by Sir John Sloane; (f) an ancient symbol for the Godhead, now used by the United States Department of Defense to mark the location of fallout shelters; and (g) the cautionary symbol for biological hazards. The elaborate and beautiful example in figure **7.7** was found on a Pima Indian basket. The section of green pepper in figure **7.8** shows a natural example of the group.

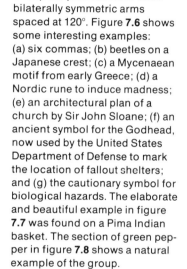

7.5a

7.5b

7.6b

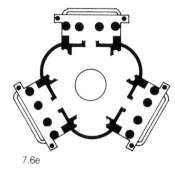

7.6e

7.6c

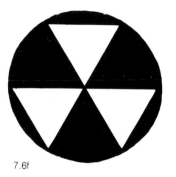

7.6f

7.6d

7.6g

7.7

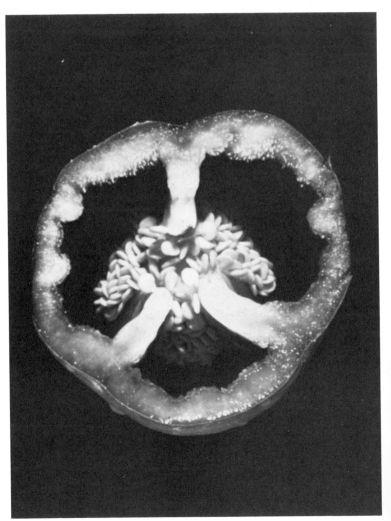

7.8

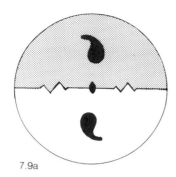

7.9a

7.10a

The Fundamental Region

Before proceeding further, we will find it useful to examine how point groups can be created from repetitions of fundamental regions.

We will define a fundamental region as the region of minimum area that can be repeated without gaps or overlaps to make a complete pattern. Shaded areas in figure **7.9** show examples of fundamental regions for groups 2, 3, 2*mm*, and 3*m*.

In frame (a) you see that the fundamental region of group 2 is half of a pie that can be rotated and joined with itself to produce a whole pie. You can use a knife bent to any shape to cut the pie as long as you make two identical cuts that meet directly in the center.

As pictured in frame (b), the fundamental region of group 3 is a third of a pie made by identical cuts of any shape that are separated by 120°. Three such pieces make a whole pie.

When mirrors join groups 2 and 3, however, the fundamental region takes a different form. No longer must the region repeat by

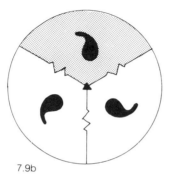

7.9b

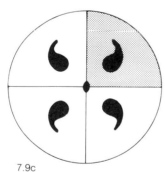

7.9c

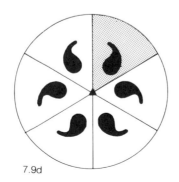

7.9d

rotation alone. It can also repeat by reflection. As illustrated in frames (c) and (d), the fundamental regions for groups 2*mm* and 3*m* are a fourth and a sixth part of the pie. Note that these pieces are bounded by straight cuts that are the mirror lines.

We shall see that mirror lines—whether in point groups, line groups, or plane groups—always mark the boundaries of fundamental regions. This fact is worth knowing because repetition of the fundamental region is often a practical way to develop a pattern.

Exercises

1. Do any letters of the alphabet exhibit threefold symmetry? Which come close?

2. Use the letters p and q to generate a 3*m* design.

3. What is the fundamental region of the two-headed bird in figure 5.4b?

4. What is the fundamental region for the section of walnut in figure 6.10?

5. Draw fundamental regions for each of the patterns in frames (a) and (b) of figure **7.10**. How do the areas of the regions compare?

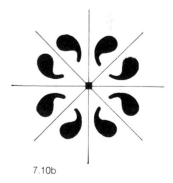

7.10b

8
The Swastika and the Greek Cross: Groups 4 and *4mm*

Group 4

As symbolized by the solid diamond in figure **8.1**a, fourfold rotation characterizes the pattern of group 4. Any two identical lines that radiate from the rotocenter and are separated by 90° mark the boundaries of the fundamental region—the region of minimum area that can be repeated to obtain the whole pattern.

It is easy to forget the strength of the feelings that were aroused in early peoples by symbols such as these. Today if we are conscious of symbols at all, we find them only vaguely pleasant or unpleasant. We view them as aesthetic expressions. We do not share the feelings of dread, well-being, or power that they once inspired. An exception, perhaps, is the Nazi swastika in figure **8.2**d. For most of us, it endures as more than just another fourfold rotocenter. It leaps from the page with a life and power of its own. We can be certain that before the age of writing and codified laws, graphic symbols like the swastika affected primitive people just as strongly. Aspirations, fears, and magical thinking all found expression in these powerful and often secret designs.

8.1a

Figure 8.1
(a) group-4 arrangement of commas
(b) design from Columbia showing four monkeys
(c) Chinese swastika design
(d) Pueblo Indian design from New Mexico
(e) plan for apartments by Frank Lloyd Wright

8.1b

8.1d

8.1c

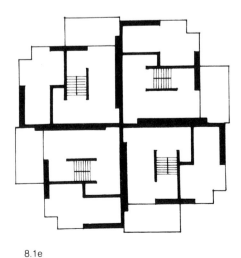

8.1e

8.2a

The Swastika

Another point about the emotional content of symbols is that the same symbol can have different meanings in different cultures. Not all swastikas, for example, have Nazi overtones. The word swastika, comes from the Sanscrit *svastika* which means "having good luck." In India the motif is a charm against evil, and in Japan it is a symbol of perfection. We surmise that the design originated independently in many cultures as an expression of a simple symmetry group. You obtain some idea of the diverse origins of the swastika from the examples in figure 8.2.

Figure 8.2
(a) Nigerian design
(b) Navaho design
(c) cramponée cross
(d) Nazi swastika
(e) pattern from Halaf, Mesopotamia
(f) design from Southern Italy, 700–800 BC
(g) Chinese, 1700–1800
(h) Chinese, about 1900
(i) Japanese
(j) design from Rhodes, ancient Greece

8.2b

8.2c

8.2d

8.2g

8.2i

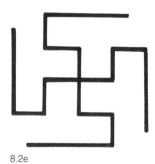

8.2e

8.2h

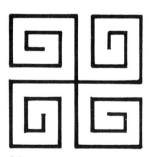

8.2j

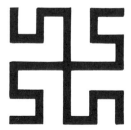

8.2f

Group-4 designs without strong overtones of the swastika appear in figure **8.3**. All show intertwining.

Figure 8.3
(a) Nigerian design
(b) American Indian, Southern Appalachia
(c) Tunisian pattern
(d) interlaced cross
(e) Ethiopian strapwork design
(f) entrailed cross
(g) American Indian, Tennessee
(h) Celtic manuscript design
(i) combination of (d) and (g), 1400–1600
(j) carved marble panel, Saint Mark's, Venice, 1000–1100
(k) Japanese
(l) Celtic manuscript design
(m) Russian

8.3a

8.3b

8.3c

8.3d

8.3e

8.3f

8.3g

8.3h

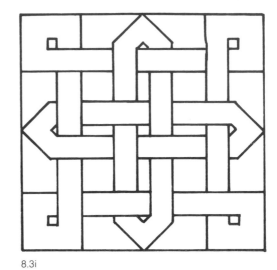

8.3i

8.3j

8.3k

8.3l

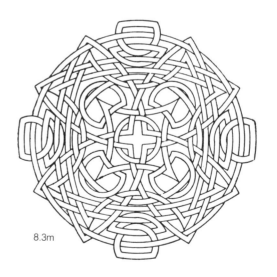

8.3m

Group 4mm

Four intersecting mirrors produce the pattern of group 4*mm*. The fundamental region is one-eighth of a circle and is bounded by mirror lines. The arrangement of commas and the basket designs in figure **8.4** show the pattern admirably. The Greek cross, which has four identical arms, represents the simplest expression of the pattern. Variations of the cross are shown in figure **8.5**.

Figure 8.4
(a) 4*mm* arrangement of commas
(b), (c), (d) Pima Indian basket designs
(e) Blackfoot Indian quiltwork
(f) Papago Indian basket design

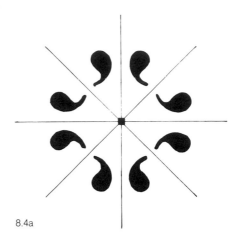

8.4a

8.4b

8.4c

8.4d

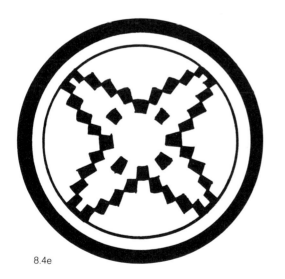

8.4e

8.4f

Figure 8.5
(a) Greek cross
(b) barbée cross
(c) fleury cross
(d) patonce cross
(e) Turkish design, sixth century
(f) ornament from the South
Pacific
(g) architectural plan by Claude-
Nicolas Ledoux.

8.5a

8.5b

8.5c

8.5d

8.5e

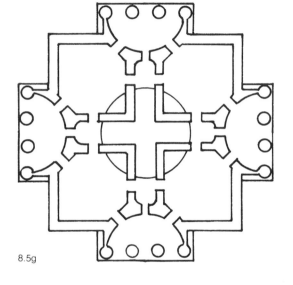

8.5g

8.5f

Two complex 4*mm* motifs appear in figure **8.6** and the forget-me-not flowers in figure **8.7** provide examples of this pattern in the natural world.

Figure 8.6
(a) Nordic rune against witchcraft
(b) Celtic manuscript design

8.6a

8.6b

8.7

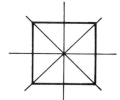

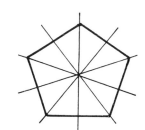

More on Mirrors

Let us return to an idea mentioned earlier, that odd-numbered and even-numbered point groups contain respectively one and two types of mirrors. In figure **8.8** we see that the equilateral triangle in frame (a), which belongs to group 3*m*, has only one type of mirror, which bisects both a corner and a side. In the square in frame (b), however, one type of mirror bisects opposite sides and a second type bisects opposite corners.

The same distinction occurs in frames (c) and (d). The mirrors of the pentagon in (c), which belongs to an odd-numbered group, bisect both a corner and an edge. The mirrors of the hexagon in (d), which belongs to an even-numbered group, either bisect two edges or two corners. This distinction between mirrors of one type and mirrors of two types holds for every odd- and even-numbered point group.

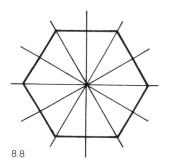

8.8

Exercises

1. Can you arrange four cards like the Jack-of-Diamonds in figure 6.1 to form a group-4 design?

2. How many repetitions of the letters b and d do you need to generate a 4*mm* design?

3. Using repetitions of the letter A, see if you can generate designs belonging to groups 1, *m*, 2*mm*, and 4*mm*.

4. To what group does the strapwork design from the Congo in figure **8.9** belong? What modification would transform it into the pattern of group 4? What modification would transform it into the pattern of group 4*mm*?

5. See if you can answer the same questions as they relate to the Celtic ornament of figure **8.10**.

8.9

8.10

9
Flowers and Pentagrams:
Groups 5 and 5*m*

Because groups 5 and 5*m* can
not combine to form groups of
greater complexity, they are not
listed with the point groups in
figure 3.1. The absence of groups
5 and 5*m* in higher-order groups
arises because fivefold rotocenters do not interact with themselves in the plane to produce
additional centers of rotation.
(This interesting and significant
fact is discussed further in the
appendix.)

Group 5
Figure **9.1** shows examples of the
fivefold rotational symmetry that
characterizes group 5: (a) a pattern of commas; (b) a flower with
petals that overlap one another
like the blades of a fan; (c) a
stylized flower motif from Japan;
(d) an interlocked joint of five ribs
in the structure of a dome; and (e)
the plan for a mortuary designed
by Frank Lloyd Wright.

9.1a

9.1c

9.1b

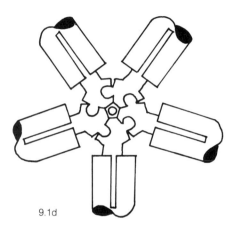

9.1d

9.1e

Interlaced variants appear in
figure **9.2**. Frame (a) depicts an
interlaced pentagram; frame (b)
shows a design for the United
States Bicentennial; and frames
(c) and (d) show Japanese crest
designs.

9.2c

9.2a

9.2b

9.2d

9.3b

Group 5m

The symmetry of five intersecting mirrors, which characterizes group 5m, is illustrated in figure **9.3**: (a) five pairs of commas; (b) an Apache basket design; and (c) a Japanese crest motif. The fundamental region of the pattern is a 36° sector bounded by mirror lines.

9.3a

9.3c

Many examples of 5*m* can be found in natural forms. Figure **9.4** shows a starfish. Figure **9.5** shows the various stages in the development of the apple which carry the imprint of 5*m* symmetry: (a) apple blossoms; (b) the sepals of a blossom after fertilization; and (c) a slice through the ripened fruit.

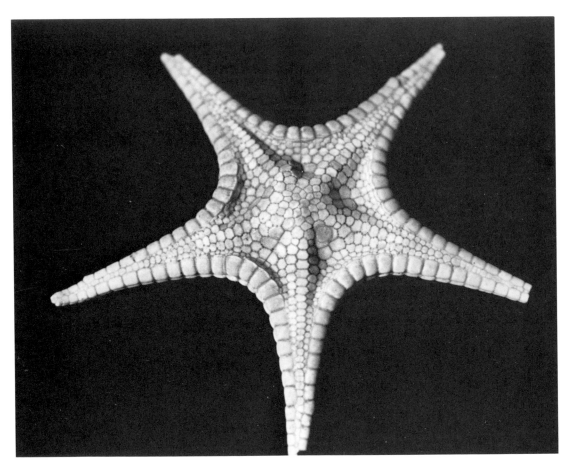

9.4

9.5a

9.5b

9.5c

Figure **9.6** shows another natural phenomenon, the apparent orbit of the planet Venus on the supposition that the earth is at rest. When viewed from the earth, represented by the center dot, the planet Venus is seen to swirl across the sky in symmetrical loops. [58: p. 154]

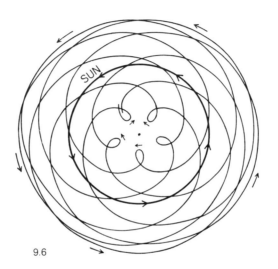

9.6

Figure **9.7** pictures the pentagram. It symbolized the secrets of mystical brotherhood to the Pythagoreans, the godhead to the Druids, a witch's foot to Celtic priests, a goblin's cross to medieval priests, and the five Mosaic books to the Jews. It would have prevented the devil from entering Faust's study except that Faust did not quite complete the diagram—he neglected to close one angle, and Mephistopheles crept through.

On many flags the five-pointed star still finds favor. The symmetrical arrangement of five stars exhibited in figure **9.8** is the insignia worn by the General of the United States Army.

9.7

9.8

10
Solomon's Seal and Snowflakes: Groups 6 and 6*mm*

Group 6

In frame (a) of figure **10.1**, six commas rotate about a small hexagon, the conventional symbol for a sixfold rotocenter. The ribs of the Gothic window in frame (b) also rotate about a common center. Both patterns belong to group 6.

The best-known example of hexagonal symmetry is the Magen David or Star of David, the symbol of Judaism. The motif, also known as Solomon's seal, is depicted in figure **10.2**a. Frame (b) of the figure shows a Russian variant of the same design, and frame (c) shows a Persian variant from the thirteenth century. Figure **10.3** displays complex examples of intertwining. Frame (a) is a Turkish dish design from the sixteenth century; frame (b) is from Russia.

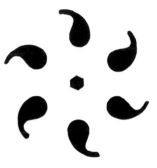

10.1a

10.2a

10.1b

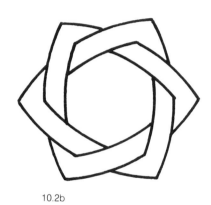

10.2b

10.2c

10.3a

10.3b

Group 6*mm*

The intersection of six mirrors produces the 6*mm* pattern illustrated in figure **10.4** by (a) commas, (b) an Arabian tile design, and (c) an Apache basket design. Whereas the fundamental region for group 6 is a 60° sector of arbitrary shape with two identical sides, the fundamental region for group 6*mm* is a 30° sector bounded by straight mirror lines.

The hexagonal snowflake belongs to group 6*mm*. Every snowflake is different, and yet each maintains the same hexagonal symmetry. As a reminder of all the beauty that nature so freely creates and destroys, the sketch in figure **10.5** shows a single flake that happened to be observed before it melted. Every moment of every day in the earth's atmosphere a myriad of these exquisite hexagonal designs come into being and pass away.

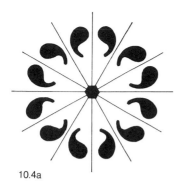

10.4a

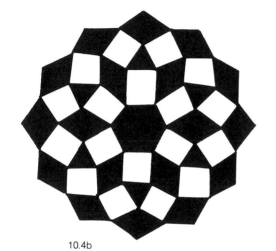

10.4b

10.4c

10.5

11
Stars and Circles:
Point Groups of Higher
Order

Groups 1, 2, 3, 4, 6 and *m*, 2*mm*, 3*m*, 4*mm*, and 6*mm* combine readily with one another to form groups of greater complexity. Groups 5 and 5*m* play no part, nor do point groups of an order higher than 6. Because of their limited combinatorial properties, therefore, we will review here only a few designs.

Groups 7 and 7m
Point groups of order *n* where *n* is a prime number greater than 5 do not occur frequently. Having a prime number of rotations, they do not subdivide into simple and more easily comprehensible patterns. Thus you find only a few examples of groups 7 and 7*m*, such as (a) the Pueblo basket design, (b) the mystic star, and (c) the eighteenth-century pattern from the Netherlands shown in figure **11.1**.

Groups 8 and 8mm
Groups 8 and 8*mm* occur with greater frequency. Their horizontal and vertical axes show them to be close relatives of groups 2, 2*mm*, 4, and 4*mm*.

11.1a

11.1b

11.1c

Figure 11.2
(a) Germanic symbol for the medieval Vehmic law courts
(b) Japanese family crest design
(c) Russian interlaced star
(d) Mimbres Indian pottery design
(e) Papago Indian basket design
(f) design from Ubangi, Central Africa

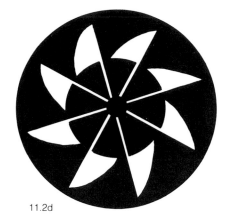

11.2a

11.2d

11.2b

11.2e

11.2c

11.2f

Figure **11.3**
(a) interior of dome of Saint
Lorenzo (1668), Turin, Italy,
designed by Guarino Guarini
(b) Chinese pattern
(c) design from India
(d) Apache basket design

11.3a

11.3b

11.3c

11.3d

Higher Order Groups

Illustrative of groups 9 and 9*m* in figure **11.4** are (a) the Chinese lattice design for a circular window, and (b) the interlaced star once popular as a symbol for the Holy Spirit. Figure **11.5** shows a sketch of the Italian city of Palmanova which dates from the fourteenth and fifteenth centuries. Figure **11.6** shows a starfish with nine arms.

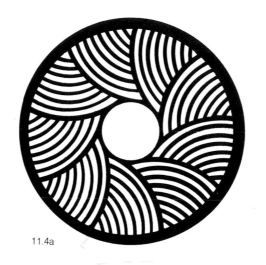

11.4a

11.4b

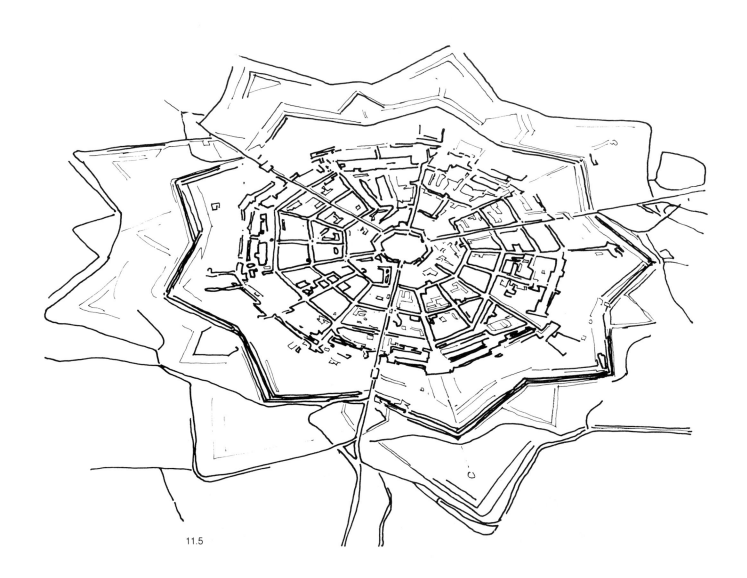

11.5

11.6

In figure **11.7**a the cross section of a modern facsimile of a Doric column shows ten interlocked wood strips in the group-10 arrangement. The design from West Africa in frame (b) belongs to group 10*mm*.

Figure **11.8** displays an intricate Russian design that belongs to group 12. Although an oval, Michelangelo's design pictured in figure **11.9** for the paving of the Capitol in Rome has an obvious affinity to group 12*mm*.

Group 13*m* is represented in figure **11.10** by a field of stars similar to that used in the early United States flag to symbolize the thirteen original colonies. The rose window of Notre Dame in Paris shown in figure **11.11** illustrates group 16*mm*.

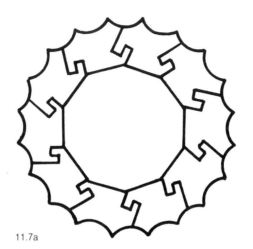

11.7a

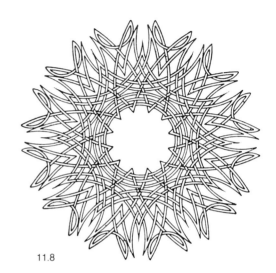

11.8

11.7b

11.9

11.10

11.11

Groups 24 and 24*mm* appear in figure **11.12** in the form of (a) a Russian interlaced star and (b) a Graeco-Roman mosaic from Ostia, Italy.

And so the list continues. Examples of rotational symmetry are legion. Every wheel with spokes, cogs, or paddles represents a point group. The group of highest or infinite order is the circle, which has complete rotational symmetry. It was therefore considered by the ancient Pythagoreans and others throughout history to symbolize eternity, unity, completeness, and perfection.

11.12a

11.12b

Exercises

1. What are the fundamental regions of the flower in figure 9.1b and the starfish in figure 9.4?

2. Can you develop a group-*m* design from duplicate images of the eight-pointed star of figure 11.2c if the images are separated by a translation?

3. To what groups do images generated in the above example belong?

4. Can you generate a group-*m* design using two nine-armed starfish like the one in figure 11.6?

5. Generate a 5*m* pattern that combines five repetitions of the letters p, q, b, and d.

III
The Seven Line Groups

. . . the repetition of the same
pattern side by side produces
another or several others.

Owen Jones

Line Groups

No Reflections	t	t2				
Centers on Mirrors	tm	t2mm				
Mirrors and Glides	mt	t2mg				
Glide Reflections	tg					

Point Groups

1	m	2	2mm	3	3m	4	4mm	6	6mm

Plane Groups

No Reflections	p1		p2		p3		p4		p6	
Centers on Mirrors		pm		p2mm		p3m1		p4mm		p6mm
Mirrors and Glides		cm		p2mg	c2mm		p31m	p4gm		
Glide Reflections		pg		p2gg						

12.1

A module is not the expression of a motif but the expression of an architectural principle.

Louis Kahn

12
Ducks in a Row:
Group *t*

We can now combine the operations of translation, reflection, and glide reflection with the point groups to create all the linear band ornaments—the seven line groups—and the two-dimensional coverings of a surface—the seventeen plane groups.

To make the line groups we will join translations, reflections, and glide reflections to groups 1, *m*, 2, and 2*mm*. Four line groups come into existence when the operations join with point groups 1 and *m*, and three line groups arise when the operations unite with point groups 2 and 2*mm*. Designations of the line groups are shown in figure **12.1**.

Group *t*

The simplest band ornament is the translation group of group *t*. It arises from successive translations of an asymmetric motif, that is, from successive shifts of a group-1 motif. The commas in figure **12.2** establish the prototype. They sit like ducks in a row, or like the lines of birds, dolphins, monkeys, dogs, or sentries in figure **12.3**.

You can imagine these patterns as extending indefinitely in each direction, to the right and to the left, and realize that the whole line of images translates. The line is like an infinitely long worm that inches forward the length of a translation so that in its new position it looks like it did in its old position.

In each pattern the length of the translation extends from one point to the next equivalent point. In figure 12.3f, for example, it extends from the eye of one bird to the eye of the next bird, or from the tip of one beak to the tip of the next beak. Of course, whether you measure between eyes, beaks, tails, or feathers, the translational distances are identical.

12.2

Figure 12.3
(a) Inca design, pre-Columbian
Peru
(b) Egyptian, New Empire period
(c) design from Panama
(d) Nazca design, Mexico
(e) American Indian quill em-
broidery from Delaware
(f) Celtic, eighth century
(g) Persian

12.3a

12.3b

12.3c

12.3d

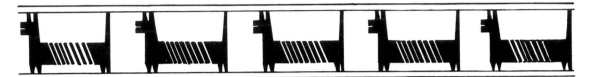

12.3e

12.3f

12.3g

The Fundamental Region

The fundamental region—the smallest portion of the pattern that repeats so as not to leave gaps or overlap with itself—is bounded by two lines of the same shape separated by a distance of one translation. Figure **12.4** portrays through shading several arbitrary fundamental regions of the pattern in figure 12.3b. The left-hand shading shows a whole dolphin and is probably the most straightforward expression of the fundamental region. However, each of the other shadings also pictures a complete, though fragmented, dolphin. You can prove this somewhat surprising assertion by rearranging the elements that lie within each shading. You will discover that each shading shows only one example of every repetitive point.

12.4

Examples

Figure **12.5** shows fronds of
Cycas revoluta, a primitive seed-
bearing plant. The abstract floral
forms in figure **12.6** exhibit the
same translational symmetry.

Figures **12.7** and **12.8** depict
wave and scroll forms and interlacements. All belong to group *t*.
Figure **12.9** shows a linear arrangement of houses designed by
Le Corbusier.

12.5

12.6a

Figure 12.6
(a) French, twentieth century
(b) ancient Greek
(c) Roman, Pompeii
(d) Chinese, eleventh century B.C.

12.6b

12.6c

12.6d

12.7a

Figure 12.7
(a) ancient Greek
(b) Chinese
(c) Hopi Indian
(d) Pima Indian basket design
(e) Toltec Indian design from
Tula, Mexico
(f), (g), (h) Mexican
(i) Greek, eighth century B.C.
(j) Berber design from North
Africa

12.7b

12.7c

12.7d

12.7e

12.7f

12.7g

12.7h

12.7i

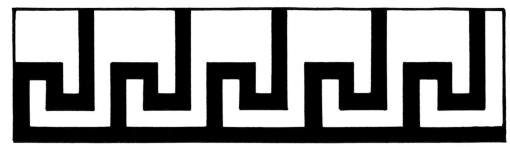

12.7j

Figure 12.8
(a) design from Borneo
(b) Celtic manuscript ornament

12.8a

12.8b

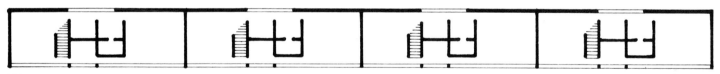

12.9

The important point for us to observe is that all these constructions and the laws connecting them can be arrived at by the principle of looking for the mathematically simplest concepts and the link between them.

Albert Einstein

13
Friday's Footprints:
Group *tg*

Another line group that arises through manipulations of group-1 images is group *tg* made by successive translations of a glide reflection. It is the pattern that Robinson Crusoe found on the beach when he discovered Friday's footprints.

Group *tg*
Figure **13.1** shows prints of the comma in the *tg* arrangement. You can see the dotted line which indicates the presence of a glide reflection and observe that the commas above and below the line form mirror images that translate in relation to one another. We would commonly say that images above and below the line have opposite-handedness. You may recall the earlier mention of the Iranian boy who dipped both hands into the paint and alternated prints of his right and left fists. Friday's feet were similarly opposite "handed," and he used them both in walking the beach—left, right, left, right.

The zipper in figure **13.2** is another common example of group *tg*. Successive teeth are opposite-handed. Those on one side cannot be transformed into those on the other side except by glide reflection.

Figure **13.3** shows examples of braiding that belong to group *tg*:

13.1

13.2

Figure 13.3
(a) Mesopotamia, ninth century
B.C.
(b) Egyptian, twelfth century
(c) ancient Greek

13.3a

13.3b

13.3c

In the realm of natural form, a succession of glide reflections establishes the alternate pattern of branching and leaf arrangement. The false Solomon's seal of figure **13.4** provides an example. Leaves on one side of the stem are mirror images of those on the other side and each leaf grows in the gap between those that grow opposite. Figure **13.5** illustrates the ways in which designers have portrayed that same pattern of growth.

13.4

Figure 13.5
(a) from India
(b) ancient Greek
(c) Egypto-Roman, third to fifth century
(d) Egyptian
(e) medieval
(f) Victorian

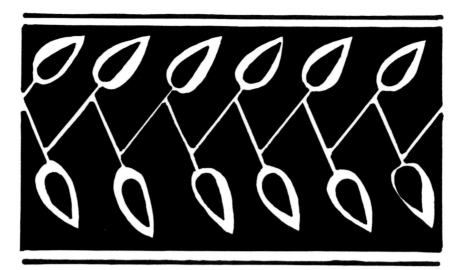

13.5a

13.5b

13.5c

13.5d

13.5e

13.5f

The Fundamental Region

The fundamental region of group *tg* is the region bounded by the line of the glide-reflection and by two arbitrary but identical lines separated by the length of a translation. Figure **13.6** shows two choices of fundamental region for the design in Figure 13.5e. In developing your own *tg* designs, you may decide not to use the fundamental region which repeats by means of glide reflection. You may choose instead to repeat by translation a region twice as large which extends across the line of glide reflection. However, identification of the fundamental region will always help you to understand the structure of a group. And group *tg* is especially worth the study. It is not as common as some of the other groups and it displays a beautifully subtle variety of repetition.

Figures **13.7** and **13.8** show abstract variations of group *tg*, and figure **13.9**, like the Chinese examples in figures **13.10**, and **13.11**, shows a collection of similar visual themes. Figure **13.12** illustrates the *tg* arrangement in plans of apartments designed by Le Corbusier for housing at Pessac.

13.6

Figure 13.7
(a) Mexican, pre-Columbian
(b) Chinese
(c), (d) modern designs of tire
treads

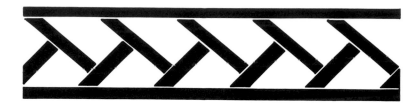

13.7a

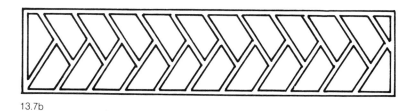

13.7b

13.7c

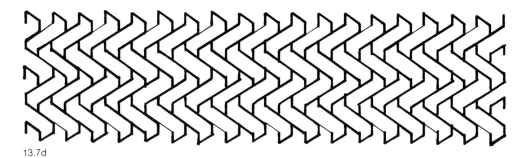

13.7d

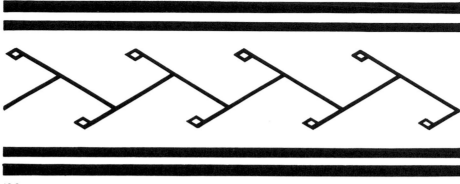

13.8a

Figure 13.8
(a) Navaho Indian
(b) Turkish design, sixteenth century
(c) medieval ornament
(d) Pueblo Indian design

13.8b

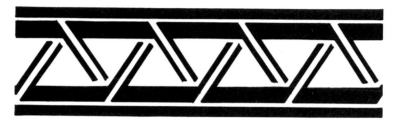

13.8c

13.8d

13.9a

Figure 13.9
(a) design from Crete, 2nd millenium B.C. Also an Arabian
and Iroquois Indian design.
(b) Caucasian rug design

13.9b

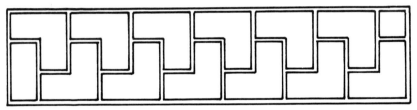

13.10a

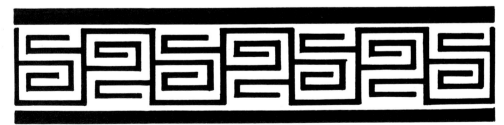

13.10b

13.11a

13.11b

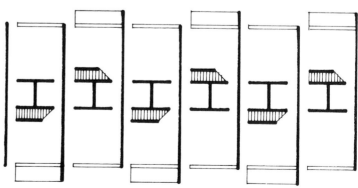

13.12

Exercises

1. Generate a *tg* band using the letters b and p.

2. What is the fundamental region of the pattern you have developed?

3. Can you illustrate a group *t* pattern with a succession of walnuts like the one in figure 6.10? (You will have to be careful not to introduce more than translation symmetry.)

4. Can you illustrate a *tg* pattern with a row of peppers like the one in figure 7.8? (Again, be careful not to introduce additional symmetries.)

5. To what groups do the patterns in frames (a) and (b) of figure **13.13** belong? Remember that in group *tg* the glide reflection must transpose the entire pattern into itself.

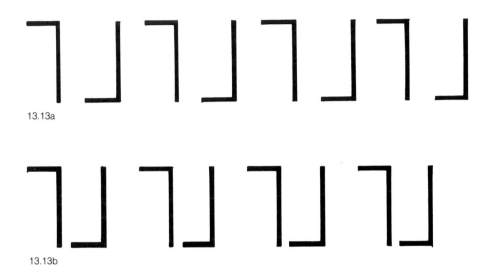

13.13a

13.13b

An image too may be
From mirror into mirror handed
on.

Lucretius

14
Reflected Reflections:
Group *tm*

To obtain groups *t* and *tg* we translated group-1 images. Working now with group-*m* images, we can generate two more line groups, groups *tm* and *mt*. Group *tm*, reviewed in this chapter, has two alternating mirror lines perpendicular to the direction of translation whereas group *mt*, reviewed in the next chapter, has a single mirror line that runs parallel to the direction of translation.

Group *tm*
Figure **14.1** shows group *tm* by means of a regular succession of pairs of commas. You can see that the commas are symmetrical about two different mirror lines. The two mirrors alternate with one another so that the commas form alternating couples: every comma points head-to-head across one mirror and tail-to-tail across the other mirror. Consequently you see that the regular translation of one perpendicular mirror produces automatically the regular translation of a second mirror that alternates with the first.

Alternatively you can generate the same *tm* pattern by placing a single comma between two parallel hand mirrors. The mirrors will reflect the image between them an infinite number of times. In exactly the same way, you will get multiple reflections of your own image when you stand between two mirrors on opposite walls. You glimpse in each mirror an endless series of images which recede into the blue-green haze of mirrored infinity. You will see that two different types of mirrors and images alternate with one another because half the images show your face and the others show the back of your head.

Each frame of figure **14.2** shows clearly the locations of the alternating mirrors that make up the *tm* pattern. One mirror passes through the center of each head, the other passes between the heads.

14.1

Figure 14.2
(a) Nazca Indian
(b) ancient Egyptian
(c) Papago Indian design

14.2a

14.2b

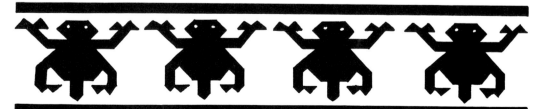

14.2c

The Fundamental Region

In group *tm* the fundamental region is bounded by two mirrors. In figure 14.2a, for example, the fundamental region constitutes exactly one half a face. Instead of repeating the fundamental region by reflection, you can repeat a region twice as large by translation. To develop figure 14.2a, for example, you can either reflect repeatedly half a face or translate repeatedly a whole face.

Figure **14.3** shows implements of war arranged in the *tm* pattern. In figure **14.4** we find conventional foliage designs from different historical periods, and in figure **14.5** some less conventional foliage patterns. Figure **14.6** shows abstract versions of the *tm* group produced by Indian tribes of North America. Figures **14.7** and **14.8** show visually related examples of *tm* ornaments from several different cultures. Figure **14.9** shows an architectural example in the design of apartment housing by Le Corbusier.

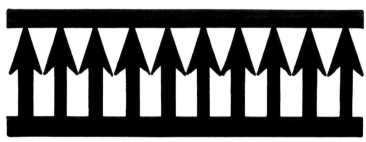

14.3a

14.3b

Figure 14.3
(a) Ghanian
(b) pre-Columbian motif from Columbia

14.4a

Figure 14.4
(a) Mesopotamian motif, first millenium B.C.
(b) ancient Egyptian
(c) ancient Greek
(d) ancient Greek

14.4b

14.4c

14.4d

14.5a

Figure 14.5
(a) design from Crete, first millenium B.C.
(b) Ceylonese
(c) Persian, seventeenth century
(d) French, seventeenth century

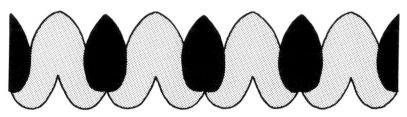

14.5b

14.5c

14.5d

Figure 14.6
(a) Navaho Indian
(b) Papago Indian
(c) Pima Indian

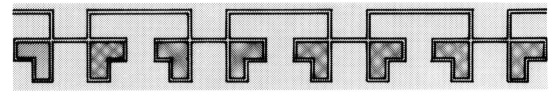

14.6a

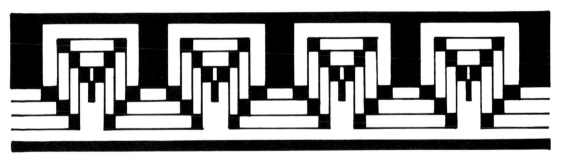

14.6b

14.6c

14.7a

Figure 14.7
(a) Egyptian, fourth millenium
B.C.
(b) Hindu

14.7b

Figure 14.8
(a) Navaho Indian
(b) ancient Egyptian

14.8a

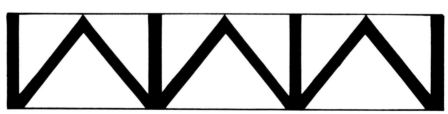

14.8b

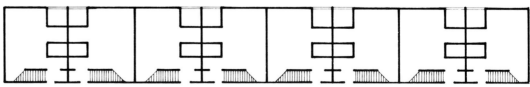

14.9

Exercises

1. Generate the *tm* pattern using the letters b and d.

2. Can you generate the *tm* pattern by successively translating a 3*m* motif?

3. What is the group designation of the Tlingit Indian design in figure **14.10**? What would be the designation if the design was not stepped, that is, if the horizontal lines ran continuously?

4. At first glance frames (a) and (b) of figure **14.11** show successions of fivefold and threefold rotocenters. Remembering that the entire pattern must be affected by every operation, what is the actual designation of those rotocenters? To what group do the two designs belong?

5. Neglecting the coloring, you would assign the designs in figure **14.12** to group *tm*. To what groups would you assign the designs if you take the colors into account, that is to say, if you consider the black commas to differ from the white commas?

14.10

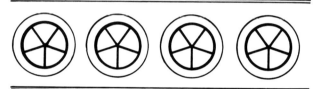

14.11a

14.11b

14.12a

14.12b

15
Reflected Sails:
Group *mt*

One way to distinguish group *tm*, described in the last chapter, from group *mt*, presented here, is to observe that group *tm* translates reflections and group *mt* reflects translations. Consequently, group *tm* contains multiple mirror lines that run perpendicular to the direction of translation and group *mt* contains a single mirror line that runs parallel to the direction of translation.

Group *mt*
The commas in figure **15.1** illustrate the *mt* arrangement. The commas form symmetric pairs about the horizontal mirror line and those pairs shift up and down the line to make an infinite string of repetitive images. You can see that the group is nothing more than a single reflection of a group *t* pattern, a reflection that makes the entire group bilaterally symmetrical.

Figure **15.2** shows *mt* relations of animal forms that have bilateral symmetry.

Figure 15.2
(a) Chinese scorpion design
(b) Inca motif, pre-Columbian
(c) Nazca Indian, Mexico
(d) Mexican

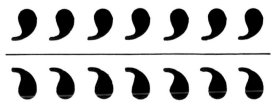

15.1

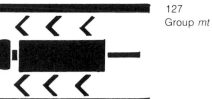

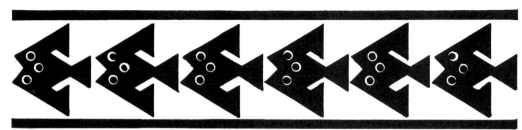

15.2a

15.2b

15.2c

15.2d

Fundamental Regions

Figure **15.3** which shows two
fundamental regions for the pattern of Figure 15.2b, reveals that
in an *mt* group the fundamental
region is bounded by a mirror line
and by two other identical lines of
arbitrary shape separated by the
length of a translation. These
fundamental regions can be
translated and reflected to
generate the whole pattern. In
order to repeat by translation
alone, you may use a region twice
as large, a region that crosses the
mirror to include two fundamental regions.

   Figures **15.4**, **15.5**, and **15.6**
show floral, wave and scroll, and
abstract variations of the *mt*
arrangement. Figure **15.7** shows
an *mt* architectural site plan
for housing designed by Le
Corbusier.

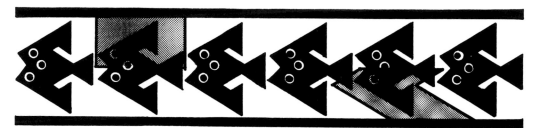

15.3

15.4a

Figure 15.4
(a) ancient Greek
(b) ancient Roman
(c) Victorian
(d) Oklahoma Indian

15.4b

15.4c

15.4d

15.5a

Figure 15.5
(a) ancient Greek
(b) Roman, fifth century
(c) Roman
(d) Greek vase design
(e) Mexican
(f) Greek vase design

15.5b

15.5c

15.5d

15.5e

15.5f

Figure 15.6
(a) Navaho Indian
(b) pattern from India
(c) Egyptian
(d) Chinese

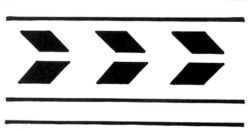

15.6a

15.6b

15.6c

15.6d

15.7

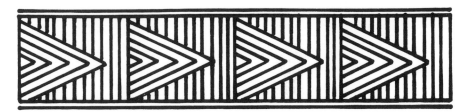

15.8a

Different Cultures

Figure **15.8** shows three strikingly similar examples of the *mt* pattern—each with an apparently independent origin: (a) design from the Sandwich Islands, (b) Persian ornament, and (c) Maricopa Indian design. Figure **15.9** presents another surprising comparison. The image in (a) was produced in Victorian England, whereas (b) was developed by the Haida Indians of the northwestern United States. Again we see that different cultures produce similar designs—not because they copy one another but because the number of symmetry groups is limited and designs within the same group tend to look alike.

15.8b

15.8c

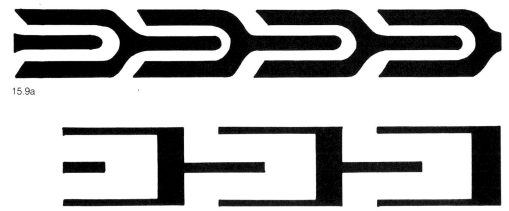

15.9a

15.9b

Exercises

1. Illustrate both the *tm* and *mt* patterns with repetitions of the letter A.

2. Illustrate groups *tg* and *mt* with repetitions of the letters q and d.

3. Indicate a fundamental region for the Maricopa design in figure 15.8c. Can you translate two of those regions to generate the entire band?

4. The Victorian and Chinese patterns in figure **15.10** (a) and (b) appear to show a succession of threefold rotations. Is that true? Remember that symmetry operations must affect the whole pattern.

5. Identify the groups represented by the patterns in figure **15.11**.

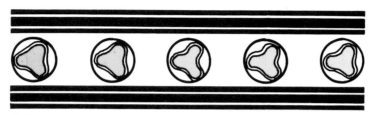

15.10a

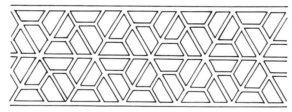

15.10b

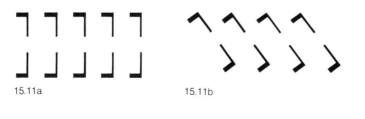

15.11a

15.11b

15.11c

15.11d

16
Grand Right and Left:
Group t2

We have completed the study of the first four line groups which incorporate elements from groups 1 and *m*. We will now investigate the three remaining line groups. They contain twofold centers, which belong to groups 2 and 2*mm*. These three line groups can be distinguished from the first four line groups that do not have rotation by the simple test of turning the entire pattern upside down. If the pattern still appears the same, it contains twofold centers.

Group t2
The simplest line group with twofold centers is group *t*2 characterized by successive translations of twofold centers. It is interesting to see in the *t*2 arrangement of commas shown in figure **16.1** that successive translations of one twofold center produces a second twofold center that alternates with the first. Do you recall the structure of group *tm*? That group is analogous to group *t*2. When a mirror is trans-

lated, group *tm* arises because a second mirror comes into existence to alternate with the first mirror. In the same way, when a twofold center is translated, group *t*2 arises because a second twofold center comes into existence to alternate with the first twofold center. You can see in figure 16.1 how one type of twofold center repeatedly leap-frogs the other to create an infinite band. The rotocenters turn their neighbors like square dancers interweaving in a grand right and left.

Figures **16.2** and **16.3** show animal and floral forms in the *t*2 arrangement.

16.1

16.2a

Figure 16.2
(a) Peruvian Nazca design
(b) Peruvian fish design
(c) Eskimo carving
(d) Peruvian monkey design

16.2b

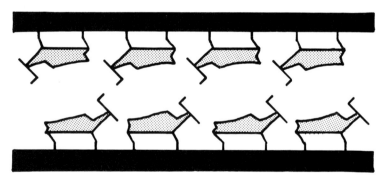

16.2c

16.2d

Figure 16.3
(a) Russian, nineteenth century
(b) French, Empire motif
(c) Caucasian rug design

16.3a

16.3b

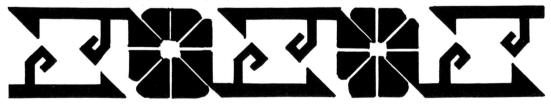

16.3c

The Fundamental Region

The fundamental region of group *t*2 can have a variety of shapes but is always bounded by lines with twofold rotation. Figure **16.4** shows how to make the construction. Through alternate points in a linear array repeat any arbitrary line with twofold symmetry. Then intersect pairs of those lines with repetitions of a third line that also has twofold symmetry. The resulting interlocked pieces will be fundamental regions.

Additional examples of the *t*2 pattern are illustrated by lines and triangles in figure **16.5**, S-forms in figure **16.6**, continuous meandering curves in figure **16.7**, Chinese swastika designs in figure **16.8**, and interlacements in figure **16.9**. A *t*2 layout for apartments is shown in figure **16.10** as designed by Frank Lloyd Wright.

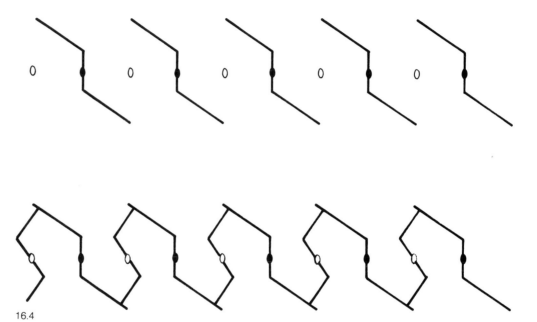

16.4

Figure 16.5
(a) simple line ornament
(b) ancient Egyptian ornament
(c) Navaho Indian
(d) Haida Indian, bear-track motif

Figure 16.6
(a) Persian carpet motif
(b) Greek, sixth century B.C.
(c) Haida Indian, shaman's hat motif
(d) Pueblo Indian
(e) Caucasian rug design
(f) Oriental design

16.5a

16.5b

16.5c

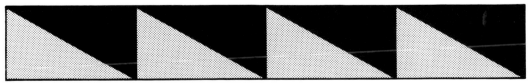

16.5d

16.6a

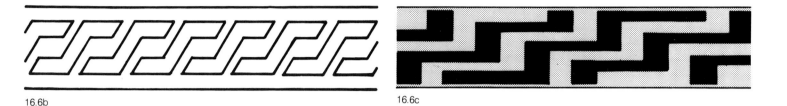

16.6b

16.6c

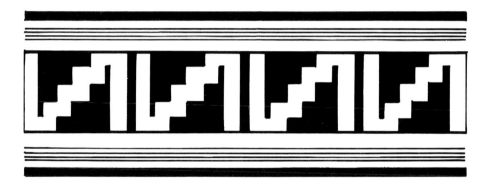

16.6d

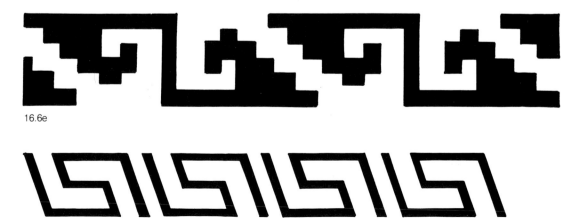

16.6e

16.6f

16.7a

Figure 16.7
(a) border design developed by
the Chinese, ancient
Greeks, and Navaho Indians
(b) ancient Greek
(c) Turkish
(d) from pre-Columbian Peru

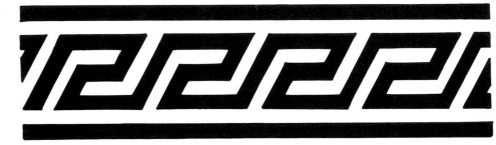

16.7b

16.7c

16.7d

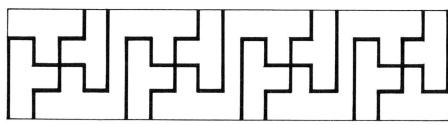

16.8a

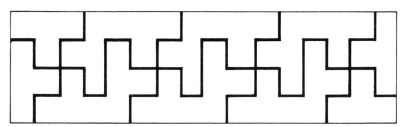

16.8b

16.8c

16.9a

Figure 16.9
(a) ancient Greek as well as Persian
(b) ancient Greek
(c) Persian
(d) Spanish
(e) design from Asia Minor
(f) Moorish
(g), (h) designs from Celtic manuscripts

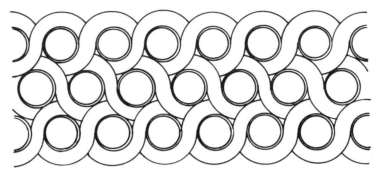

16.9b

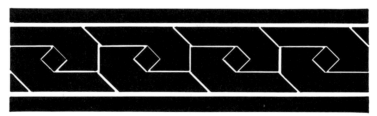

16.9c

16.9d

16.9e

16.9f

16.9g

16.9h

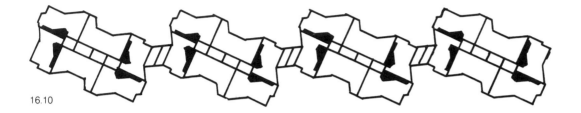

16.10

Exercises
1. Using playing cards like the Jack-of-Diamonds in figure 6.1, show two different ways to illustrate group *t*2.

2. What group is formed when bands like the one in figure 16.5b are stacked in two parallel rows, one directly above the other?

3. In the example above, does it matter if the two bands are translated relative to one another?

4. What is the group designation of the medieval design in figure **16.11**?

5. What group is produced by the succession of apparent fourfold and sixfold rotocenters in the Japanes and Italian designs of figure **16.12**? Why can a band ornament contain no higher-order rotational elements than twofold centers?

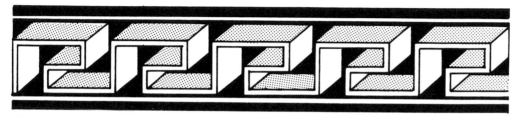

16.11

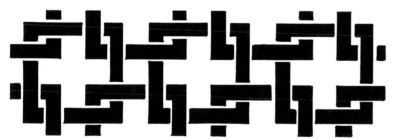

16.12a

16.12b

17
Reflected Whirls:
Group *t2mg*

Group *t2mg*

Group *t2mg* is especially inter-
teresting. It is one of the two line
groups that contains all four
symmetry operations: translation,
rotation, reflection, and glide reflection. In figure **17.1** the commas in the *t2mg* arrangement
show the interrelations of
the operations. The pattern can
be obtained in four different
ways: (1) through successive
translations of four commas, (2)
through successive rotations of a
pair of reflected commas, (3)
through successive reflections of
two commas that are immediately
adjacent to a twofold center, and
(4) through successive glide reflections of a pair of reflected
commas. You can thus verify that
group *t2mg* contains within itself
line groups *t*, *t2*, *tm*, and *tg*.

The prehistoric Indian design
from Delaware in figure **17.2**
shows a dramatic example of
group *t2mg*. See if within it you
can find translations, rotations,
mirror reflections, and glide
reflections. Notice how the presence of the twofold centers al-
lows the entire band to maintain
the same appearance when it is
turned upside-down.

The Fundamental Region

What is the fundamental region of
the *t2mg* pattern? We see in figure 17.2 that it contains half of a
bird and half of the adjacent vertical stripe. The fundamental region is therefore bounded by a
mirror line and a line with twofold
rotational symmetry. If you wish
to make the *t2mg* pattern by
translation alone, you must repeat a region with four times the
area of the fundamental region.

Figure **17.3** shows flowers and
leaves in the *t2mg* arrangement.
Notice that frame (d) depicts the
design we saw in figure 1. Curves,
90° angles, and 45° angles char-
acterize the *t2mg* meanders in
figures **17.4**, **17.5**, and **17.6**. It is
interesting to see the reappear-
ance of the swastika in some of
those examples. Figure **17.7**
shows *t2mg* arrangements of
separated elements.

17.1

17.2

17.3a

Figure 17.3
(a), (b), (c) ancient Greek
(d) Arabian motif, from Cairo

17.3b

17.3c

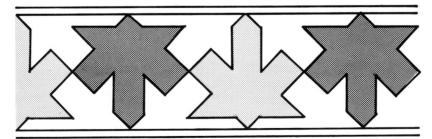

17.3d

Figure 17.4
(a) American Indian, Gulf Coast
(b) Iroquois Indian
(c) Norwegian, sixteenth century

17.4a

17.4b

17.4c

17.5a

Figure 17.5
(a) ancient Greek
(b) French, Louis XV
(c) Chinese, as well as ancient
Greek
(d), (e) Chinese

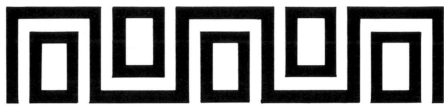

17.5b

17.5c

17.5d

17.5e

17.6a

Figure 17.6
(a) Navaho Indian
(b) Caucasian rug design, Kazak
(c) Yorok Indian design
(d) Islamic, from Egypt, sixteenth century
(e) medieval ornament

17.6b

17.6c

17.6d

17.6e

Figure 17.7
(a) Nigerian textile design
(b) site plan for attached houses,
twentieth century
(c) ornament from Pakistan, sixteenth century
(d) medieval ornament

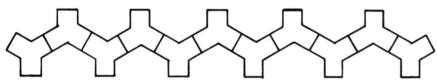

17.7a

17.7b

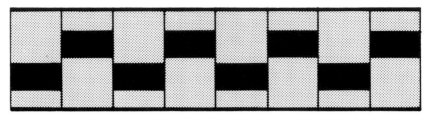

17.7c

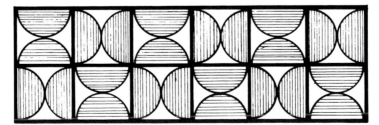

17.7d

17.8a

Coloring

Some of the most interesting ornaments are obtained by coloring just half of the *t2mg* pattern. Figure **17.8** shows some instances. When you encounter such a coloring, a moment usually passes before you realize that the top of the pattern is identical to the bottom. That recognition is likely to give you a pleasurable jolt—an ''aha!'' reaction.

Figure 17.8
(a) Russian
(b) Ghanian
(c) border design from Hadrian's villa, Tivoli
(d) Navaho Indian

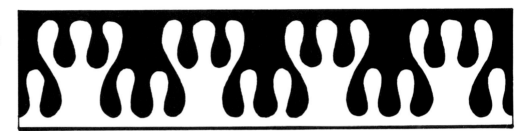

17.8b

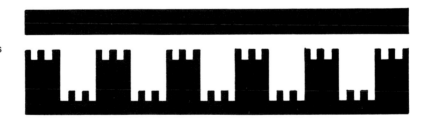

17.8c

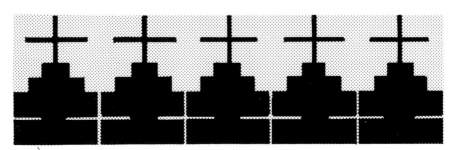

17.8d

17.9a

Exercises
The designs in Figure **17.9** might appear at first glance to belong to group *t2mg.* To what groups would you assign them?

Figure 17.9
(a) ancient Greek
(b) from Guyana, twentieth century
(c) Chinese
(d), (e) medieval
(f) Nigerian
(g) ancient Greek
(h) from Alexandria, Egypt, third-fourth centuries

17.9b

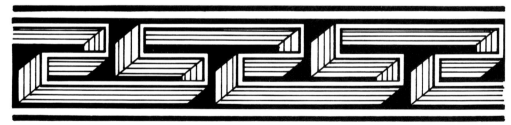

17.9c

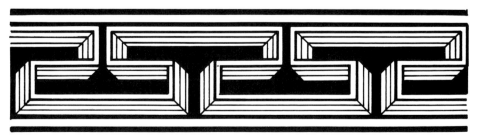

17.9d

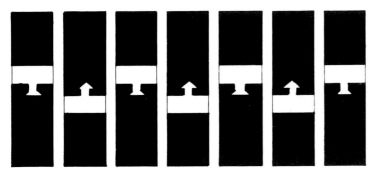

17.9e

17.9f

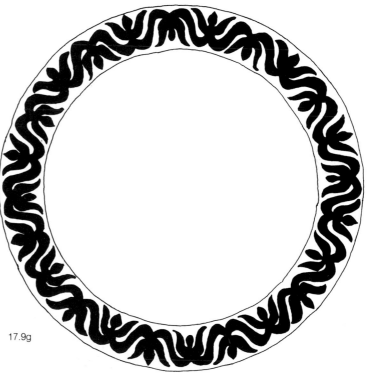

17.9g

18
Linear Kaleidoscope: Group *t2mm*

The remaining line group, *t2mm*, consists of two alternating *2mm* rotocenters. The commas in figure **18.1** illustrate the arrangement. A mirror line runs the length of the pattern as in group *mt* and two perpendicular mirrors alternate with one another as in group *tm*. The intersections of the mirrors mark the centers of two different *2mm* point groups so that one *2mm* center alternates with the other.

Mirrors
The fundamental region of *t2mm* is bounded by an open-ended rectangle of three intersecting mirrors. As a result, the fundamental region of the design in figure 18.1 contains exactly one comma. See if you can verify that the fundamental region has only one quarter of the area of the region you would repeat if you used translations alone.

You can observe the fundamental region in action by taping three mirrors together as illustrated in figure **18.2**. After you set the mirrors at right angles to one another and put a motif like a comma between them, they will reflect an infinite number of times to produce the *t2mm* pattern. It is especially instructive to change the orientation of the motif as it is being reflected. Try reflecting three-dimensional objects and exploring the results of placing the mirrors at different angles to one another.

Figure **18.3** shows *t2mm* foliage arrangements. See if you can locate the fundamental region for each design. Curvilinear, angular, and intertwined variations of *t2mm* are illustrated in figures **18.4**, **18.5**, and **18.6**.

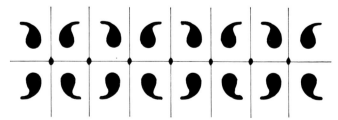

18.1

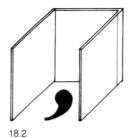

18.2

Figure 18.3
(a) ancient Egyptian
(b) ancient Greek
(c) Turkish, sixteenth century

18.3a

18.3b

18.3c

Figure 18.4
(a) Iroquois Indian design
(b) ornamental pattern from
Borneo

18.4a

18.4b

18.5a

Figure 18.5
(a) Caucasian rug design, Kazak
(b) Greek vase design
(c) Egyptian ornament
(d) Chinese

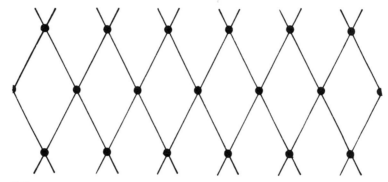

18.5b

18.5c

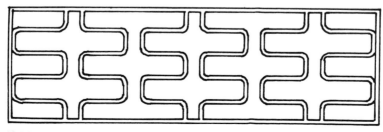

18.5d

18.6a

Figure 18.6
(a) Pompeian mosaic
(b) medieval
(c) medieval
(d) Celtic manuscript design

18.6b

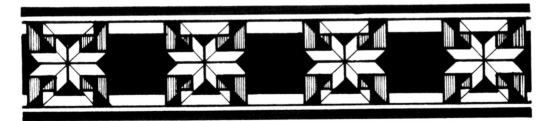

18.6c

18.6d

Twofold Centers
Figures 18.7 through 18.10 show apparent arrangements of four-, six-, eight-, and tenfold rotocenters. But as we know, since the entire band must rotate end-for-end, the highest-order rotations in the figures are twofold and all the examples belong to group *t2mm*.

Figure **18.7**
(a) Victorian ornament
(b) Arabian
(c) Pompeian mosaic
(d) Byzantine mosaic

18.7a

18.7b

18.7c

18.7d

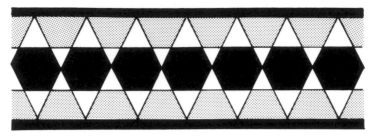

18.8a

Figure **18.8**
(a) Pompeian mosaic
(b) Chinese lattice design,
seventeenth century

Figure **18.9**
(a) Chinese lattice design,
seventeenth-eighteenth century
(b) Arabian

Figure **18.10**
(a) carved ivory panels in a
wooden door, from Cairo, fourteenth century

18.8b

18.9a

18.9b

18.10

18.11

Exercises

1. Illustrate group *t2mm* with repetitions of the letters b, d, p, and q.

2. What line group is generated if a group *t2mm* pattern is stacked with itself?

3. What is the group designation of only the dark portion of figure 17.8a?

4. Can you generate *t2* and *t2mg* bands by repetitions of the swastika in figure 8.2a?

5. What is the group designation of the ancient Chinese bronze ornament illustrated in figure **18.11**? To what line group do the top and bottom halves belong?

Where order in variety we see,
And where, though all things
differ, all agree.

Alexander Pope

19
Recapitulation

A Useful Summary
We have come quite a distance. We have combined the four operations of translation, rotation, reflection, and glide reflection to generate some of the common point groups and all seven line groups. Figure 12.1 on page 95 provides a useful summary of these groups. When you study that figure, note that each of the seven line groups is positioned directly above the point group that it contains. Thus you can see at a glance that two line groups contain point groups 1, *m*, and 2, and one contains point group 2*mm*.

With regard to operations, figure 12.1 arranges the line groups in four categories. Two line groups have no reflections, two have their centers of rotation on mirror lines, two contain glide reflections as well as mirrors, and one contains opposite-handed centers that arise through glide reflection.

In a concise way, then, the figure summarizes the makeup of the line groups, with regard to both the point groups they contain and the way in which they incorporate reflections and glide reflections. Shortly we will add the seventeen plane groups to the same chart to show how they are constructed.

Limitations
Figure **19.1** presents all the line groups. Instead of repeating a comma, figure 19.1 repeats the letter b—intermixed with letters d, q, and p—letters obtained through reflection, rotation, and glide reflection of the letter b. Consequently figure 19.1 shows all the line groups by means of symmetry operations on the letter b.

At this point you might wish to prove to yourself that only seven line groups exist. You might play with different arrangements of the letters b, d, q, and p to see whether you can discover still other line groups. Such an exercise should convince you that the possibilities of repetitive arrangement are strictly limited.

At first you might suppose that designers of band ornaments would feel hindered having to work with only seven possible arrangements. However, the work of the designer is like that of the musician who manipulates only the twelve notes of the chromatic scale to create the beauties of music. The limitations provide the discipline that an artist seeks in order to render a good performance. In *Poetics of Music*, Igor Stravinsky touched on this point when he discussed the self-imposed discipline of the fugue:

Doesn't the fugue imply the composer's submission to the rules? And is it not within those strictures that he finds the full flowering of his freedom as a creator? . . . My freedom will be so much greater and more meaningful the more narrowly I limit my field of action. . . . [60: p. 79, 68]

Group *t*	b b b b b b b b b b b
Group *tg*	b p b p b p b p b p b
Group *tm*	b d b d b d b d b d b
Group *mt*	b b b b b b b b b b b p p p p p p p p p p p
Group *t2*	b q b q b q b q b q b
Group *t2mg*	b q p d b q p d b q p
Group *t2mm*	b d b d b d b d b d b p q p q p q p q p q p

19.1

IV
The Seventeen
Plane Groups

One can hardly overestimate the depth of geometric imagination and inventiveness reflected in these patterns. Their construction is far from being mathematically trivial. The art of ornament contains in implicit form the oldest piece of higher mathematics known to us.

Herman Weyl

No Reflections	*t*	*t2*		
Centers on Mirrors	*tm*	*t2mm*		
Mirrors and Glides	*mt* *t2mg*			
Glide Reflections	*tg*			

Point Groups

1	*m*	2	*2mm*	3	*3m*	4	*4mm*	6	*6mm*

Plane Groups

No Reflections	*p1*	*p2*	*p3*	*p4*	*p6*
Centers on Mirrors	*pm*	*p2mm*	*p3m1*	*p4mm*	*p6mm*
Mirrors and Glides	*cm*	*p2mg* *c2mm*	*p31m* *p4gm*		
Glide Reflections	*pg*	*p2gg*			

20.1

Our experience hitherto justifies us in believing that nature is the realization of the simplest conceivable mathematical ideas.

Albert Einstein

20
Two Nonparallel Translations: Group *p*1

Group *p*1

The chart in figure **20.1** shows the line and point groups we have studied as well as the seventeen plane groups. Reading from the chart you discover that the *p*1 pattern contains group-1 motifs and no reflections. The stylized commas in figure **20.2** shows an example of this group. You can see that *p*1 is generated by successions of nonparallel translations, or, what amounts to the same thing, intersections of group *t* linear bands.

You frequently find *p*1 commas on Persian rugs. It is a simple and elegant pattern. A *p*1 rug looks different from different sides. It has a distinct bottom, top, right, and left. In terms of symmetry the entire rug belongs to group 1 so that only a full rotation through 360° brings it into coincidence with itself. Most rugs, of course, have a higher degree of symmetry. They belong mainly to group 2*mm*: their four corners are identical and their pattern looks the same when turned 180°.

The Lattice

Consideration of the lattice and the unit cell reveals why the group is designated *p*1. But these terms first require definition.

The dots in the *p*1 pattern of figure **20.3**a call attention to a set of equivalent points, which in this example mark the tips of the commas' tails. Such a collection of equivalent points is called a lattice. If you transfer the lattice points to tracing paper and shift them across the pattern, taking care to keep their angular orientation the same, they will fall on other sets of equivalent points. Frame (b), for instance, shows an example of the lattice superimposed on a different portion of the pattern and, as in frame (a), you can see that all the points are equivalent.

20.2

20.3a

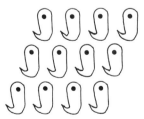

20.3b

The Unit Cell

Figure **20.4** shows how you can connect the lattice points with sets of parallel lines to create parallelograms. Each parallelogram in frame (a) has the same shape and content, and each can be successively translated to generate the entire pattern. Because the parallelogram is the smallest cell that can reconstitute the pattern under translation, it is called a unit cell. Furthermore, it is called a primitive unit cell, and designated *p*, because it contains only one complete lattice point—the point at the corners, or more precisely the four pieces of a point at the corners.

The other frames of figure 20.4 illustrate different ways to connect the points of the lattice in order to obtain differently shaped unit cells. All the parallelograms have the same content and area, though differently shaped; all are primitive unit cells, and under translation all of them will generate the lattice.

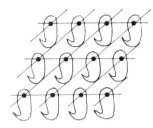

20.4a

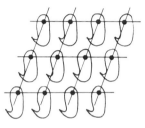

20.4b

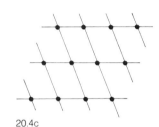

20.4c

More on Designations

The designation $p1$ reveals that the corners of the primitive cell p mark points with group-1 symmetry. Later when we draw the lattices of groups $p2$, pm, and pg, we will find that the corners of primitive cells fall on twofold centers, mirrors, and glide lines—that is to say, on elements 2, m, and g. We will thus use the same procedure to identify each plane group. The designation will indicate the symmetry at the corners of the unit cell.

Unit Cells and Fundamental Regions

After this discussion about the unit cell, can you recall the definition of a fundamental region? It is the smallest piece that can repeat to make the pattern. Do you think that the fundamental region and the unit cell are the same? Your answer should be no. The fundamental region can repeat by rotation, reflection, and glide reflection as well as by translation. In contrast, the unit cell can repeat only by translation. Furthermore, the fundamental region can have any shape that joins with itself, whereas the unit cell must be either a parallelogram or a hexagon. Later we will see that

the unit cell frequently contains more than one fundamental region.

In the $p1$ pattern, however, the unit cell just happens to be a fundamental region. This coincidence occurs because translations alone produce the pattern. Even in the $p1$ pattern, however, the fundamental region can have shapes other than a parallelogram or hexagon, so while the unit cell is a fundamental region, a fundamental region may not be a unit cell.

Examples of $p1$

Figures 20.5–20.10 show animal forms arranged in the $p1$ pattern. The whales and birds in figure **20.5** were produced by the Chilkat Indians of southern Alaska and the Nazca Indians of Peru.

In figure **20.6** the artist M. C. Escher created a background of flying horses that interpenetrated with those in the foreground. Neglecting the difference in color, the horses in the background and foreground are identical, so that the fundamental region consists of only a single horse. The pattern is an exotic jigsaw puzzle in which every piece has exactly the same shape.

20.5a

20.5b

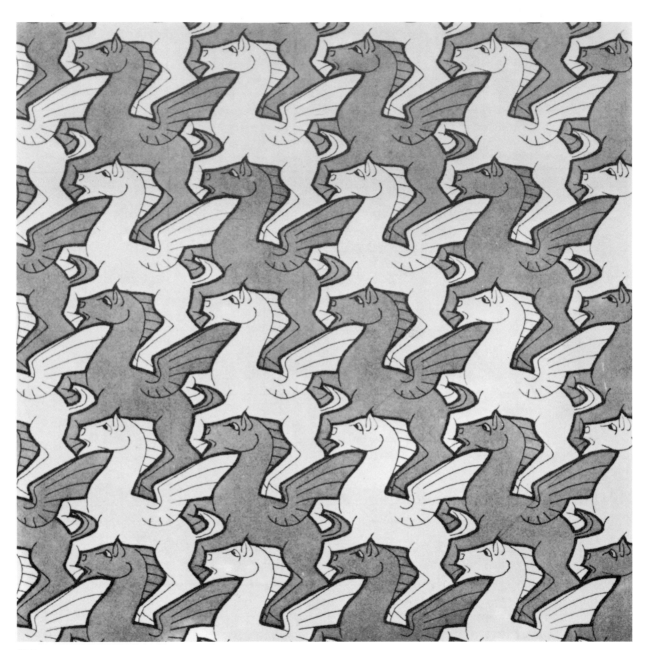

20.6

As shown in figure **20.7**a the unit cell of the pattern contains the area of one horse but has the shape of a square—a special case of a parallelogram. As illustrated in frames (b) and (c), you can connect equivalent points to create other sets of parallelograms, and you can see that each parallelogram contains the parts of a complete horse.

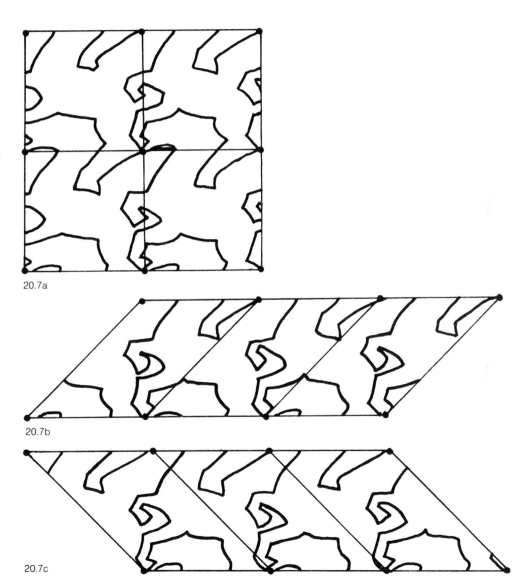

20.7a

20.7b

20.7c

In figures **20.8** and **20.9** which illustrate more of Escher's work, the fundamental region consists of a bird combined with a fish. The unit cell is a parallelogram in figure 20.8 and a rectangle—another special case of parallelogram—in figure 20.9. Figure **20.10** shows four different fundamental regions for the design of figure 20.8, that is, four different ways to combine the bird and fish to make a single piece which under translation can join with itself to fill the plane.

20.8

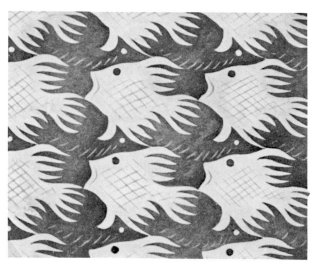

20.9

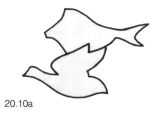

20.10a

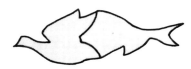

20.10b

20.10c

20.10d

Creating Your Own Fundamental Regions

How difficult is the creation of such interlocking patterns? Probably both easier and more difficult than you imagine. It is easy to obtain a pattern made from a single interlocking piece, but difficult to develop the piece so that it looks like a natural form. To draw a piece that interlocks with itself, start with a parallelogram (a square or rectangle is permitted) and modify opposite sides in exactly the same way. Figure **20.11** reveals the process. You then add to the bottom the area taken from the top, and to the left side you add the area taken from the right side. The resulting piece is a fundamental region which will fit with itself to fill the plane without gaps or overlaps. You are likely to find the development of these interlocking pieces a fascinating game.

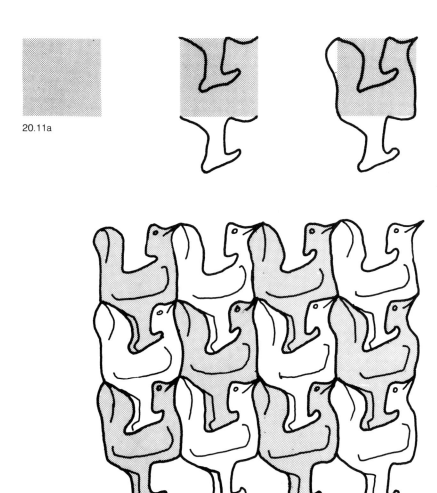

20.11a

20.11b

Traditional Patterns
Figures 20.12–20.15 show floral, spiral, and abstract forms which illustrate traditional variations on the *p*1 pattern.

Figure **20.12**
(a) cotton printer's block, India, nineteenth century
(b) modern French

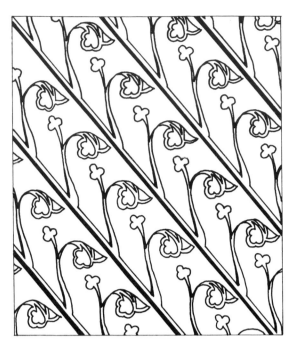

20.12a

Figure **20.13**
(a) Egyptian, seventh century B.C.
(b) Greek, sixth-fifth century B.C.
(c) Indian design from the south-eastern United States
(d) Chinese

20.12b

20.13a

20.13b

20.13c

20.13d

Figure **20.14**
(a) appliqué quilt design, United
States, 1875

Figure **20.15**
(a) Inca, pre-Columbian Peru
(b) Valiente Indian bag, Panama

20.14

20.15a

20.15b

Exercises

1. Figure **20.16** shows how an array of parallelograms can be subdivided to form an array of hexagons. Do the parallelograms and hexagons have equivalent areas?

2. Using figure 20.16 as a guide, see if you can convert the array of parallelograms in figure 20.4a to an array of hexagons. (Note that the lines of the hexagons are composed of parts of the long diagonal of a single parallelogram and parts of the short diagonals of two double-sized parallelograms.) Satisfy yourself that any array of parallelograms can be similarly subdivided.

3. Convert an array of squares to hexagons.

4. Treating identically the opposite sides of each hexagon in an hexagonal array, show how you can obtain *p*1 packings of irregular hexagons. Are these irregular hexagons fundamental regions? Are they unit cells?

5. Locate a unit-cell hexagon in the center of figure 20.7a. Does it contain the components of a single horse?

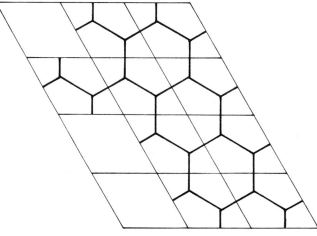

20.16

21
Two Parallel
Glide Reflections:
Group *pg*

Group *pg*
The chart of figure 20.1 indicates
that group *pg* contains glide
reflections of group-1 motifs. Figure **21.1** illustrates the arrangement with commas. Two sets of
parallel glide lines alternate with
one another; one set passes between the heads of the commas
and the other passes between the
tails. These glide lines are spaced
equally and run vertically up and
down to form *tg* bands. Group *t*
bands run horizontally.

Primitive Cells
If you connect equivalent points
at the head of each comma as in

figure **21.2**, you obtain a lattice
whose unit cells are either
rectangles or parallelograms. The
rectangle is the preferred alternative because its sides are more
nearly equal in length. Figure **21.3**
shows points of the lattice
superimposed on the pattern
so that corners of unit cells,
whether rectangles or parallelograms, fall on glide lines. The
position of lattice points
gives group *pg* its name: it contains a primitive cell *p* whose
corners fall on lines of glide reflection *g*.

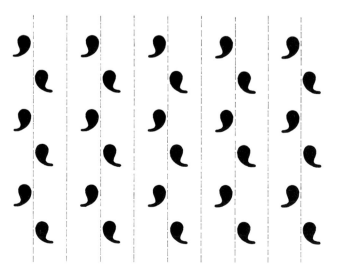

21.1

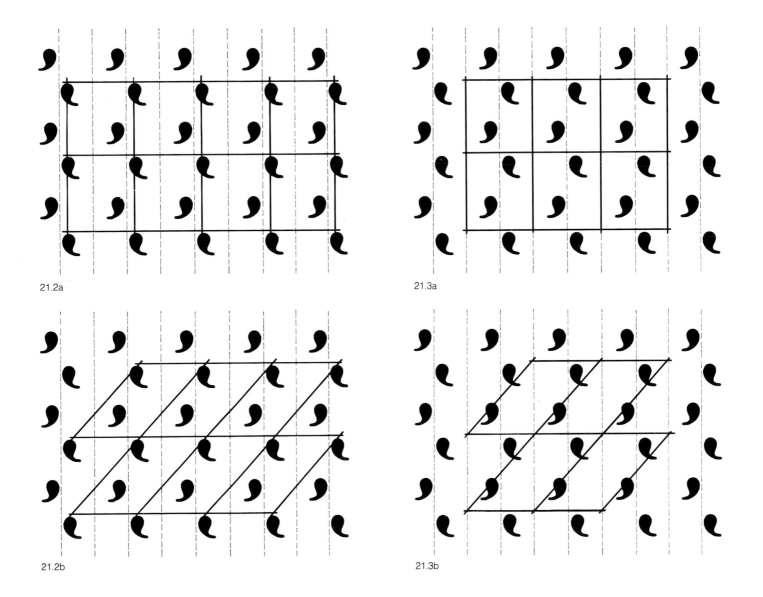

21.2a

21.3a

21.2b

21.3b

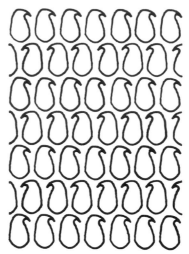

Examples of *pg*

You frequently see the *pg* pattern of commas on oriental rugs. Figure **21.4** shows a representative example in which all the commas crowd together to fill each other's gaps.

Figures 21.5–21.7 show *pg* foliage patterns and abstract designs.

Figure **21.5**
(a) cotton printer's design, India, nineteenth century
(b) prototypical branching design
(c) modern French

21.4

21.5a

21.5b

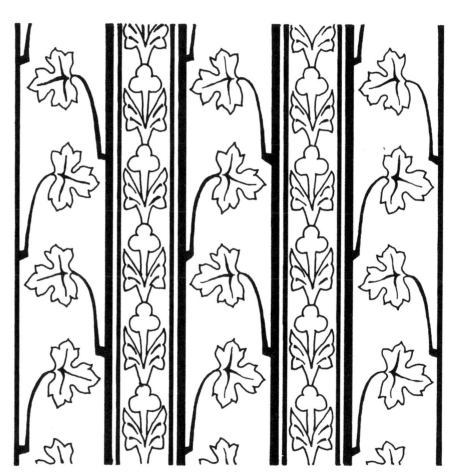

21.5c

Figure **21.6**
repetitions from a cylindrical
stamp, Mexico

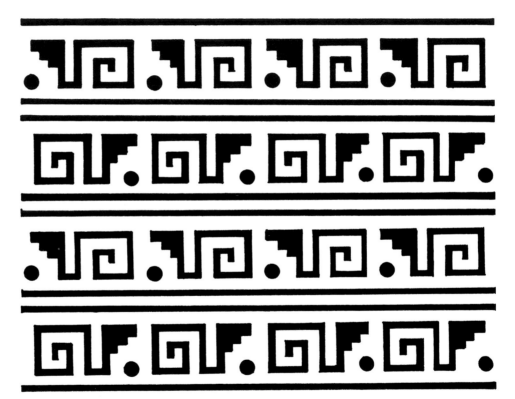

21.6

Figure **21.7**
(a) design from the Congo
(b) modified design from a Celtic manuscript

21.7a

21.7b

Figure **21.8** presents a Peruvian design that uses animal motifs in a *pg* arrangement. It is interesting to compare this design with those of M. C. Escher in figure **21.9.** Escher's designs also show a *pg* repetition of animal motifs but the animals interlock without gaps or overlaps, so that if you neglect color, the background and foreground figures are identical. Each swan and knight is a fundamental region that joins with itself to make the entire pattern.

21.8

21.9a

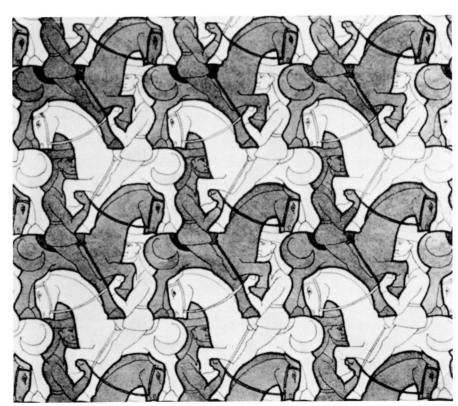

21.9b

21.10a

How to Draw Fundamental Regions

What are the constraints on these fundamental regions? We can use the *pg* arrangement of commas to find out. Figure **21.10**a shows the commas, the glide lines, and the rectangular unit cells with each unit cell split into two fundamental regions. These regions repeat horizontally by translation and vertically by glide reflection. Frame (b) shows another choice for the fundamental region. Each region in frames (a) and (b) encloses only one comma and has an area of one-half a unit cell. Each region glide reflects vertically along two different lines and translates horizontally.

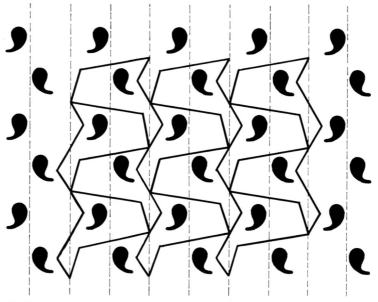

21.10b

You can develop Escher-like *pg* patterns in a straightforward manner. Simply interconnect with a single line any three corners of a parallelogram. Figure **21.11**a gives an example. You can then alternate horizontal bands composed of direct translations of the line with horizontal bands composed of mirror images of the line. Additional refinement produces the high-steppers of figure 21.11b.

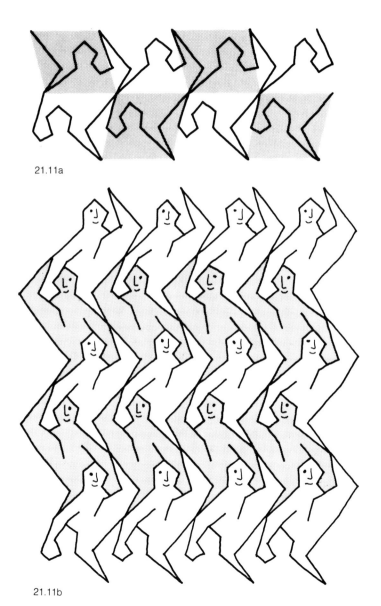

21.11a

21.11b

22
Two Parallel Mirrors:
Group *pm*

Group *pm*

Group *pm* contains rows of *tm* bands stacked directly above one another so that translations occur parallel to two alternating and equally spaced mirror lines. Figure **22.1** shows commas in the *pm* arrangement. As indicated by solid lines, one set of mirrors runs between the heads of the commas and the other runs between the tails. Lattice points can be chosen so that corners of rectangular unit cells fall on mirror lines. One is shown shaded in the figure.

Probably the easiest way to generate this pattern is to draw a band with symmetry *t* and reflect it in two hand mirrors held parallel to the band on each side. Reflections between the mirrors will produce a *pm* group.

Figure **22.2** illustrates the *pm* arrangement with a fleur-de-lis pattern and two designs from ancient Egypt. The floral patterns in figure **22.3** have the same symmetry as do the more abstract designs of figure **22.4**.

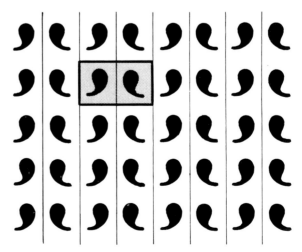

22.1

22.2a

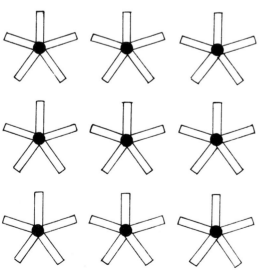

22.2b

22.2c

Figure 22.3
(a) Egypto-Roman, first-third century
(b) ancient Egyptian
(c) design from India

22.3a

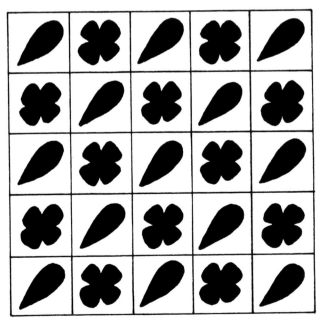

22.3b

22.3c

Figure 22.4
(a) ancient Egyptian
(b) Sandwich Islands

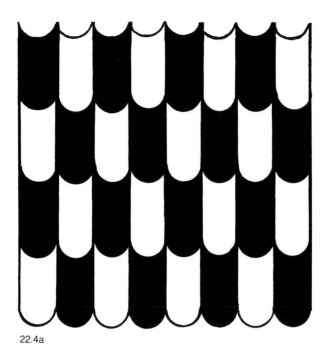

22.4a

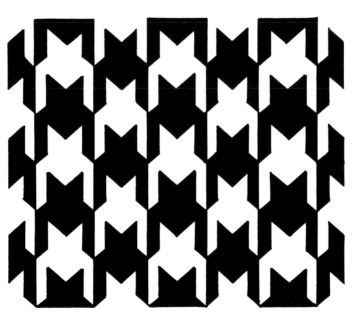

22.4b

The Fundamental Region

The fundamental region of the *pm* pattern has one-half the area of a unit cell. It is bounded on two opposite sides by mirror lines and its two remaining sides are translations of one another. Figure **22.5** shows by shading fundamental regions for the designs in figure 22.4. Figure **22.6** shows a *pm* group in which each flag is a fundamental region.

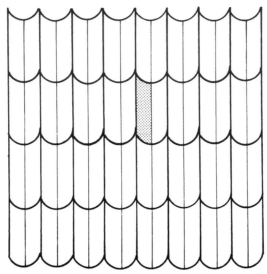

22.5a

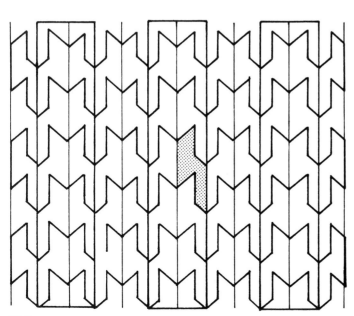

22.5b

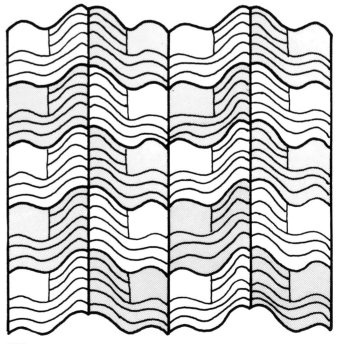

22.6

Exercises

1. You can easily arrange group *m* motifs to form a *pm* arrangement. Can you arrange the same motifs to form a *pg* arrangement?

2. Show how the pentagram of figure 9.7 can serve as a motif in *p*1, *pg*, and *pm* arrangements.

3. Figure 21.2a shows an array of rectangular unit cells for the *pg* pattern. Can you convert that array to an equivalent array of hexagons? How many commas does each hexagon contain?

4. Find both a rectangular and a hexagonal unit cell in figure 22.5b.

5. What is the group designation of the design in figure **22.7**? Does the pattern contain mirrors or glide lines?

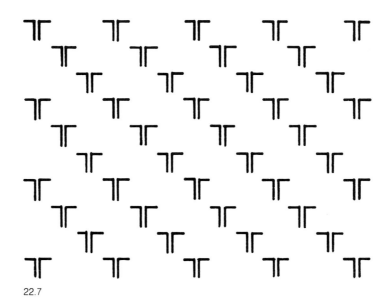

22.7

It's most remarkable that order
can be the same for everyone and
design can be so different.

Louis Kahn

23
A Reflection and a
Parallel Glide Reflection:
Group *cm*

Group *cm*

Group *cm* is a staggered form of group *pm*. The stagger occurs along lines of glide reflection between the mirror lines. If you compare the commas in figure 22.1 which show the *pm* group with those in figure 23.1a which show the *cm* group you will see the effect of the glide lines. Also compare the motifs in figure 22.2 with those in figure 23.4.

Repetitive Cells

Within the *cm* pattern you can isolate three different types of repetitive cell: (1) the fundamental region, (2) the primitive unit cell *p*, and (3) the centered unit cell *c* from which the group gets its name.

Examples of fundamental regions appear in frames (b) and (c) of figure **23.1**. Mirror lines bound them on the sides and a line that is glide-reflected bounds them on the top and bottom so that they reflect in horizontal rows and glide reflect in vertical columns.

The Rectangular Cell

Figure **23.2** shows examples of primitive unit cells which have twice the area of a fundamental region. They generate the *cm* pattern through translation alone. Because the corners of the primitive cells fall on mirror lines, the group could receive the designation *pm*. However, because we already have a group called *pm*, and more importantly, because the primitive cell is not rectangular and therefore easy to translate, a non-primitive rectangular cell is conventionally chosen. Figure **23.3** shows an example. This nonprimitive cell is designated *c* because it has a lattice point at its center. You can verify that it contains four times the area of a fundamental region and twice the area of a primitive cell. Since the corners and center of cell *c* fall on mirror lines *m* the conventional designation for the group is *cm*.

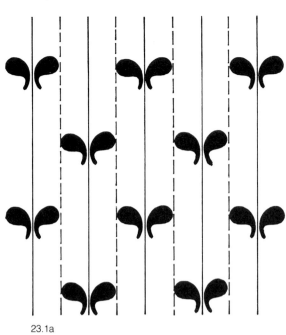

23.1a

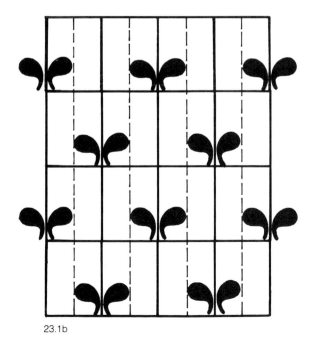

23.1b

23.1c

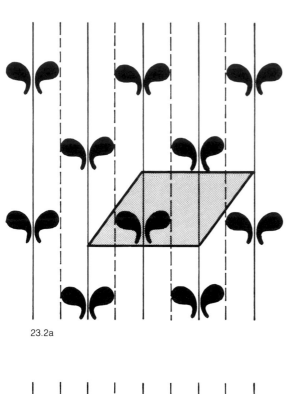

23.2a

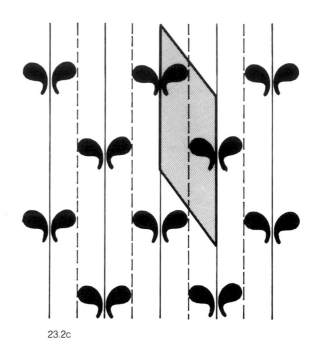

23.2c

23.2b

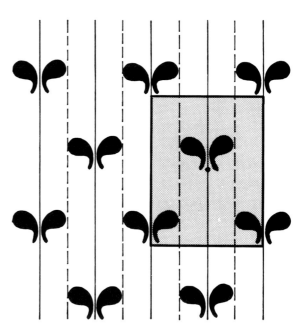

23.3

As already indicated, the *cm* designs in figure **23.4** use the same motifs as the *pm* designs in figure 22.2. In figures **23.5–23.7** floral and abstract elements further illustrate the *cm* arrangement.

Figure 23.4
(a) medieval design
(b) ancient Egyptian

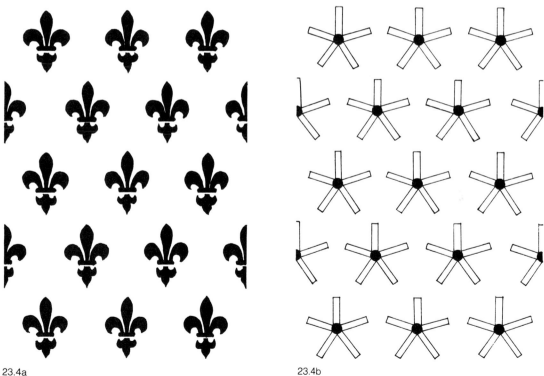

23.4a

23.4b

Figure 23.5
(a) prehistoric, New Mexico
(b) design from a Phoenician
tomb, Syria,
first millenium B.C.
(c) Pine Tree quilt pattern from
Massachusetts,
1875–1900

23.5a

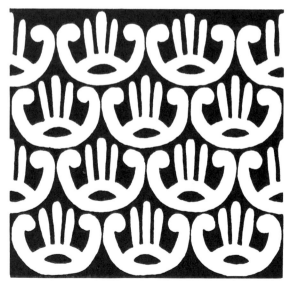

23.5b

23.5c

Figure 23.6
(a) Japanese design, nineteenth century
(b) Chinese
(c) Chinese, 1850

23.6a

23.6b

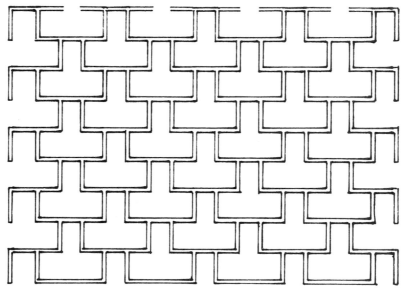

23.6c

Figure 23.7
(a) American Indian, northeast
region
(b) Byzantine
(c) American Indian, southwest
region

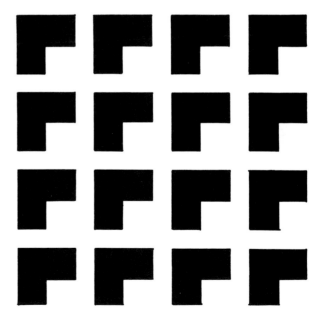

23.7b

23.7a

23.7c

Figure **23.8** shows (a) an early
Mesopotamian design and (b) a
Moorish design in the Alhambra
in Spain. It happened that after
M. C. Escher visited the Alhambra
and carefully copied the design in
figure 23.8b, he produced the *cm*
pattern of beetles in figure **23.9**.

Figure 23.8
(a) Mesopotamian, first millenium
B.C.
(b) Moorish design, Alhambra

23.8a

23.8b

23.9

23.10a

Fundamental Regions

Since each of Escher's beetles has bilateral symmetry, it encompasses two fundamental regions rather than one. However, you can make interlocking *cm* patterns that use a single fundamental region as the generating motif. In three steps figure **23.10** shows how: (1) draw any line between two parallel mirror lines (2) glide reflect the line to produce a *tg* band, and (3) successively reflect the band. When treated in this fashion, the line and mirrors in frame (a) generate the outlines of the birds in frame (d).

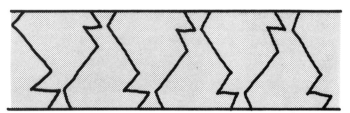

23.10b

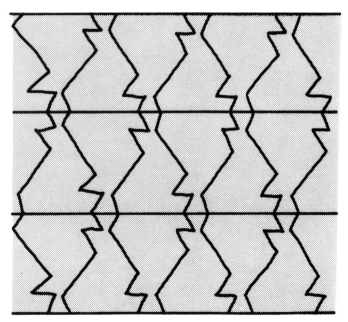

23.10c

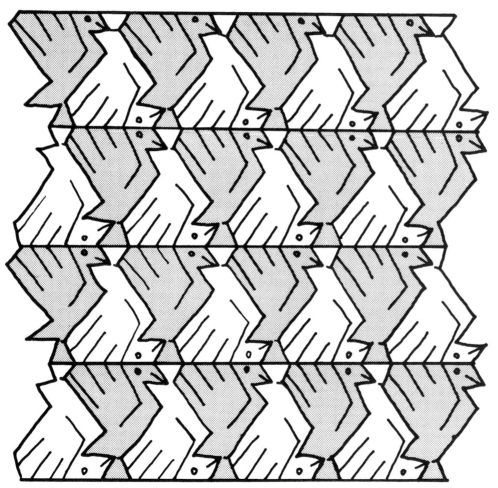

23.10d

Exercises

1. At first glance figure 23.7c looks like a *p*1 arrangement. Why isn't it?

2. Using the motif in figure 23.7, generate *p*1, *pm*, and *pg* arrangements. (The *pg* arrangement will be the most difficult. Be careful to avoid reflections.)

3. What is the arrangement of the black areas alone in figure 22.4b?

4. What is the arrangement of the black areas alone in figure 23.10d?

5. Outline in figure 23.6b a fundamental region, a primitive unit cell *p*, and a centered cell *c*.

24
Four Half-Turns:
Group *p*2

Having examined the four plane
groups that contain no rotational
elements, let us now consider
groups that have rotation. Five
plane groups have twofold and
only twofold rotation. Their designations are listed in figure 20.1.
Three of them have twofold centers without mirrors and two of
them have twofold centers with
mirrors, that is to say, three of
them contain group-2 centers
and two of then contain 2*mm*
centers. All five groups, however,
share the following characteristics: each looks the same when
turned 180°; each contains repetitions of four different twofold
centers; every twofold center of
the same type has the same
orientation; and any point that
bisects the line joining two identical centers marks the site of
another twofold center.

Group *p*2

The commas in figure **24.1** picture group *p*2, one of the five
groups that contains twofold rotations. In the figure the ovals
with the four distinguishing
marks indicate the sites of the
four different twofold centers.
Those rotocenters form a net. As
you can see in figure **24.2**a, each
corner of every mesh within the
net is studded with a different
type of twofold center. An example of a mesh is indicated by
shading in figure 24.2a.

In making *p*2 designs you will
find it useful to know the relation
of a mesh to a unit cell and to a
fundamental region. As an illustration, figure 24.2b shows a unit
cell within the *p*2 pattern. Its corners fall on equivalent points that
are repetitions of the same
twofold rotocenter. Consequently you can see how group
*p*2 receives its name: it contains a
primitive unit cell, *p*, whose corners lie on the same type of
twofold center, 2. When you
compare figures 24.2a and 24.2b
you see that the unit cell has four
times the area of a mesh.

What about the fundamental region? It turns out to have twice the area of a mesh and consequently half the area of a unit cell. Whereas the mesh has the shape of a parallelogram and the unit cell has the shape of a parallelogram or a hexagon, the fundamental region can have any shape that joins with itself under 180° rotations to cover the plane.

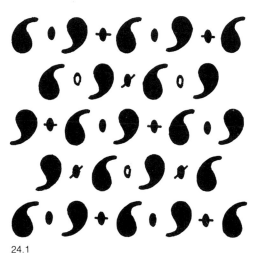

24.1

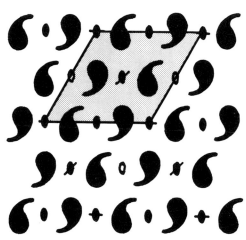

24.2b

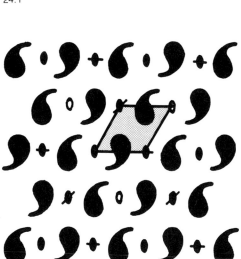

24.2a

Fundamental Regions
Figure **24.3** outlines a basic way to draw the fundamental region for a *p*2 pattern. Arrange nine dots to mark the corners, the center, and the center of each edge of a unit cell. (Although a rectangular cell is illustrated here, you can use any type of parallelogram.) Now repeat at the top and bottom of a cell a line that has twofold rotation. At the left and right sides of the cell, repeat a different line that also has twofold rotation. After you add another line with twofold rotation through the center of the cell, you will obtain a pair of fundamental regions related to one another by a half-turn. Translation of the pair of regions in figure 24.3d produces the outlines of the birds in figure **24.4**.

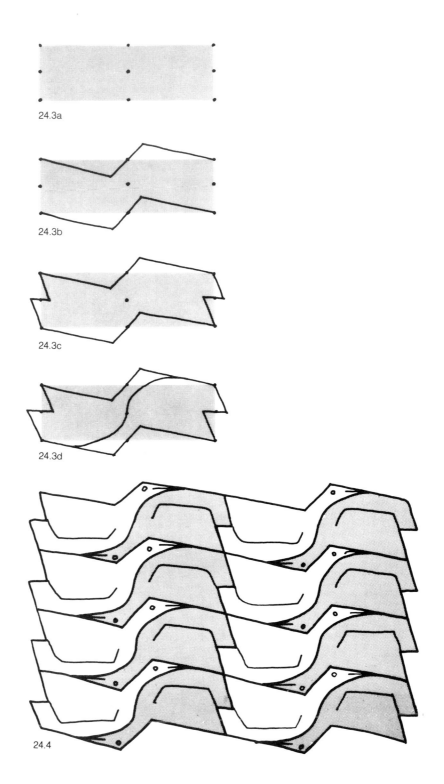

24.3a

24.3b

24.3c

24.3d

24.4

Examples

Historical examples of the $p2$ arrangement appear in figures 24.5–24.10. Frame (a) of figure **24.5** shows a straightforward stacking of $t2$ bands that inevitably generates a $p2$ plane group. In contrast, frame (b) portrays an inseparable $p2$ interlacement. Figures **24.6** and **24.7** show stackings of regular modules and figure **24.8** illustrates $p2$ arrangements of S-forms. Figures **24.9** and **24.10** depict interlocked animal motifs. If you analyze the fundamental region of a single fish in figure 24.10 you will see that it can be developed in accord with the procedure outlined in figure 24.3.

Figure 24.5
(a) ancient Egyptian design
(b) Coptic tapestry motif, Egypt

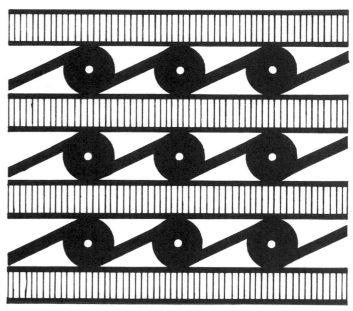

24.5a

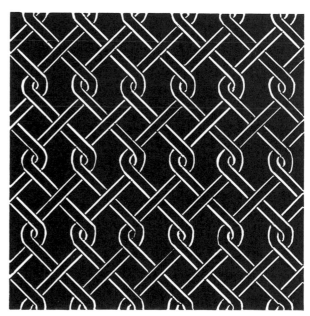

24.5b

Figure 24.6
(a) brickwork pattern
(b) brickwork pattern

Figures 24.7
(a) and (b) Chinese lattice designs

24.6a

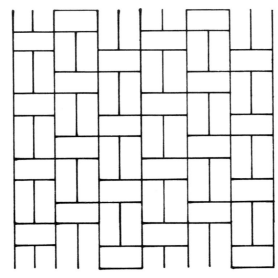

24.6b

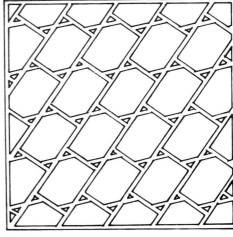

24.7a

24.7b

24.8a

Figure 24.8
(a) ancient Greek, sixth century
B.C.
(b) Hohokam Indian design,
Arizona, A.D. 1000
(c) Italian ceramic motif, twentieth century

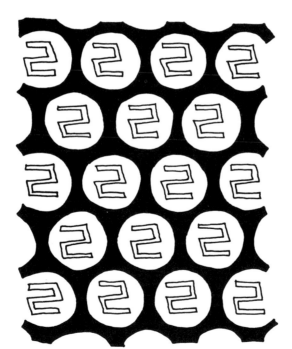

24.8b

24.8c

24.9a

Figure 24.9
(a), (b), (c) Peruvian textile designs

24.9b

24.9c

Figure 24.10
(a) design by M. C. Escher

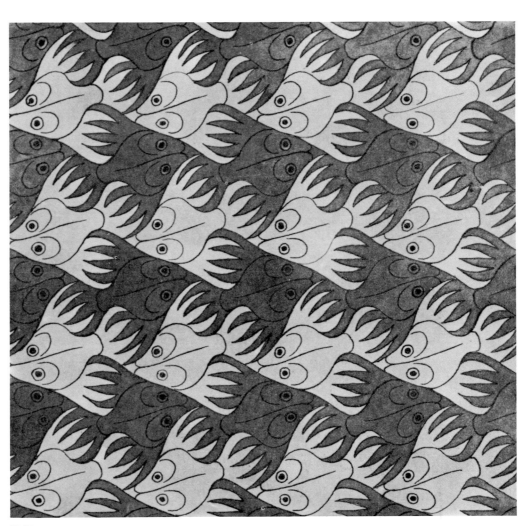

24.10

Exercises

1. What plane group do you generate by stacking the band ornament illustrated in figure 16.5b?

2. Find a mesh, a fundamental region, and a unit cell in the design of figure 24.8c.

3. The *p2* pattern can be generated by manipulating only three instead of four different twofold rotocenters. The fourth center develops naturally after you specify the others. You can easily prove this for yourself. Simply reproduce a motif by rotating it around three twofold centers. Can you see the fourth center emerge on its own?

4. What is the group designation of the line ornaments in figure **24.11**? How many of those line groups do you find in frame (e) which pictures a Chinese brickwork design from the Han dynasty?

5. To what groups do the designs in figure **24.12** belong? (The pattern in frame (b) is from India.)

24.11a

24.11b

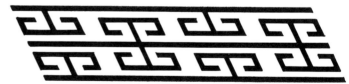

24.11c

24.11d

24.11e

24.12a

24.12b

25
A Mirror and a Perpendicular Glide Reflection: Group p2mg

As described in figure 20.1, two groups of twofold centers contain both glides and mirrors. The simpler of the two is *p2mg*, illustrated with commas in figure **25.1** where parallel mirror lines intersect at right angles with parallel lines of glide reflection. Both the mirrors and glides occur in two distinct types that alternate with one another. The glides cut through the rotocenters and the mirrors pass between them.

Figure **25.2** adds shading to figure 25.1 in order to show a *t2mg* band. You can see that the entire pattern consists of successive translations of this band.

The shading in figure **25.3** shows a single rectangular mesh marked at each corner by a different type of twofold center. The shading in figure **25.4** depicts a unit cell that has four times the area of a mesh. The corners of the unit cell fall on intersecting mirrors and glides.

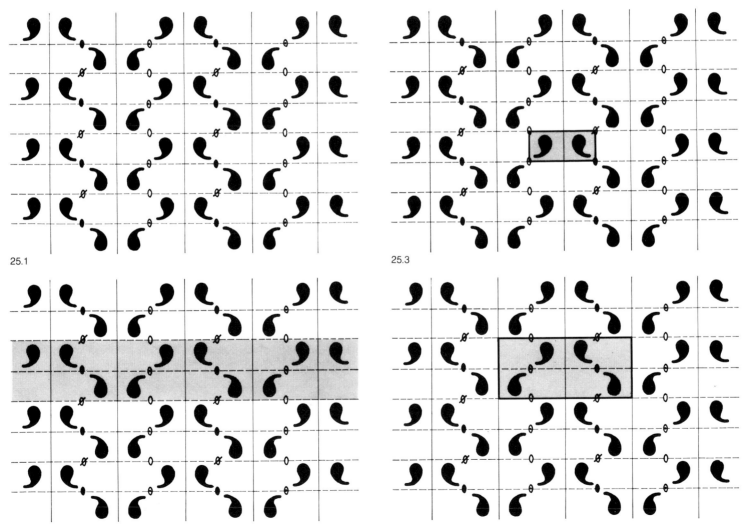

25.1

25.3

25.2

25.4

Examples of Group *p2mg*
The Nazlini American Indian design of figure **25.5** shows the *p2mg* pattern as successions of *t2mg* bands. In figure **25.6** the bands interlock with one another to produce zig-zag forms. Notice in figure **25.7** how the Chinese lattice designs break up the zig-zag and how the layout for a parking lot in figure **25.8** disrupts the zig-zag even more.

25.6a

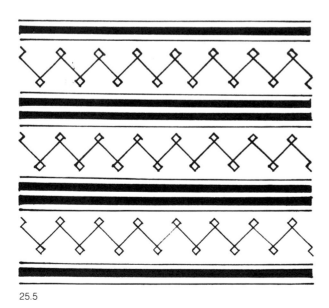

25.5

25.6b

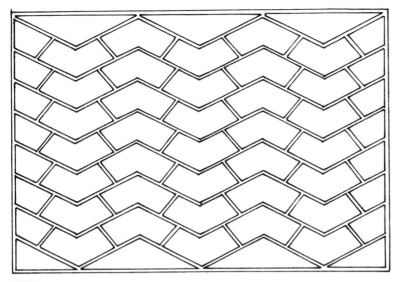

25.7a

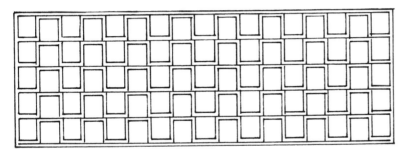

25.7b

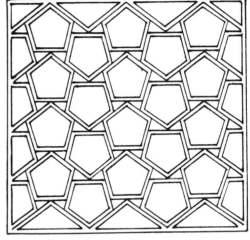

25.7c

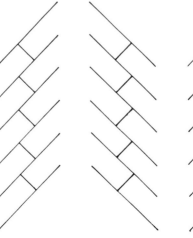

25.8

As an exercise, see if you can locate the rotocenters in each of the *p2mg* brickwork designs of figure **25.9**. You should find four different types of twofold centers in each example.

Figure **25.10** shows a striking design from Africa. Its simple interdigitations are reminiscent of the irregular pattern of the brain coral shown in figure **25.11**.

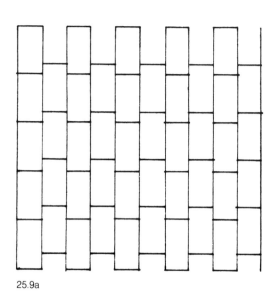

25.9a

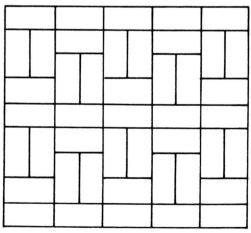

25.9b

25.9c

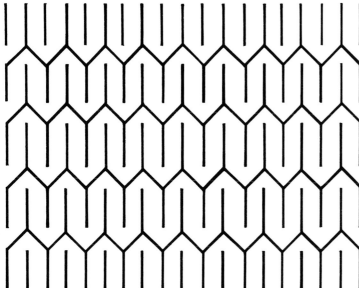

25.10

25.11

Color Reversals

The patterns in figure **25.12** are variations on the interdigitations of Figure 25.10. Note the reversals of color in each example. These reversals are elaborations of the reversals we saw in chapter 17 which described *t2mg* bands.

Figure 25.12
(a) African
(b) medieval heraldic design, vair in pale
(c) medieval heraldic design, barry-wavy
(d) Persian, early fifteenth century
(e) Persian, early nineteenth century
(f) Arabian

25.12a

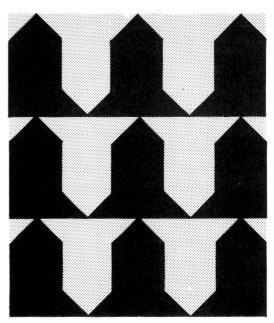

25.12b

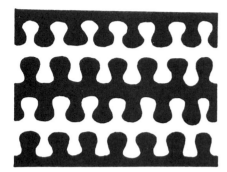

25.12c

25.12e

25.12d

25.12f

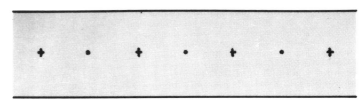

25.13a

Creating the Fundamental Region

The essential ingredients of the fundamental region of the *p2mg* pattern are two twofold rotations and a reflection. Consequently, to make patterns of fundamental regions, simply draw a row of alternating twofold centers between two mirror lines as illustrated in figure **25.13a**. Then draw identical lines with twofold rotation through one set of centers as shown in frame (b) and a different set of identical lines with twofold rotation through the other set as in frame (c). Reflecting these lines in the mirrors produces the *p2mg* outline of heads in frame (d).

At first glance the interlocked animals in the Peruvian design of **25.14** appear to illustrate the *p2mg* group. But do they? Look closely at the hands and see if you can locate twofold centers. To what group does the design actually belong?

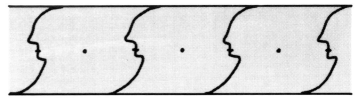

25.13b

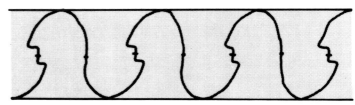

25.13c

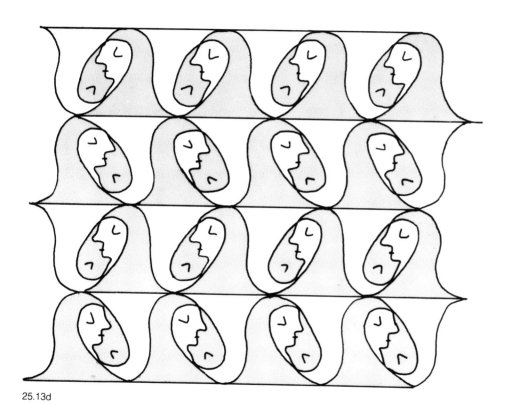

25.13d

25.14

Escher's designs in figures **25.15** and **25.16** are true embodiments of the *p2mg* pattern. Notice, however, that each crab and each fish consists of two fundamental regions. You can also see in figure 25.16 how the modification of just one type of line with twofold rotation produces several different types of fish.

25.15

25.16

*The Japanese, you know, think
of rocks as the bones of a
garden—the plants simply come
and go.*

Isamu Noguchi

26
Two Perpendicular
Glide Reflections:
Group *p2gg*

Whereas group *pg* contains glide lines that run in one direction, group *p2gg* contains glide lines that run in two directions, as demonstrated in figure **26.1**a. The glides intersect perpendicularly—two at the center of every mesh. The smaller shaded area in frame (b) reveals one of the rectangular meshes whose diagonally opposite corners fall on twofold centers that are mirror images of one another. The larger shaded rectangle is a unit cell. It has four times the area of the mesh, and its corners fall on four identical intersections of glide lines.

Examples of *p2gg*

Figure **26.2** shows designs that emphasize the twofold centers. In these designs you see S-forms that interlock with their glide-reflected images.

The *p2gg* examples in figure **26.3** seem more complicated. To analyze them, locate first the four twofold centers. Between these centers you should then be able to locate intersecting lines of glide reflection.

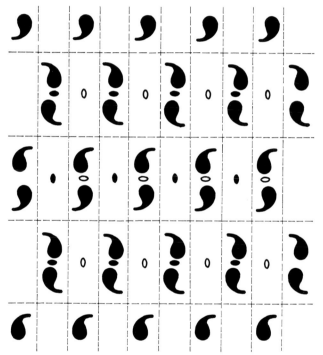

26.1a

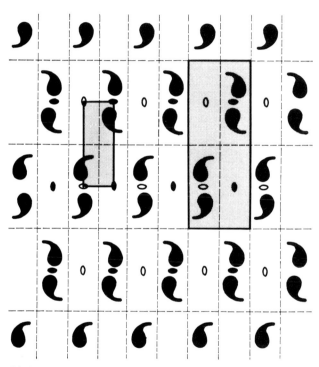

26.1b

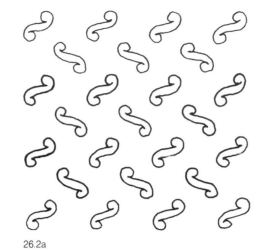

26.2a

Figure 26.2
(a) sixteenth century textile
(b) Chinese, ancient bronze,
Chou dynasty, 1100–255 B.C.
(c) Chinese lattice design

26.2b

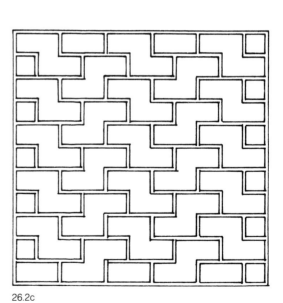

26.2c

Figure 26.3
(a) Mexican, Zapotec Indian
(b) Arabic
(c) Arabic

26.3a

26.3b

26.3c

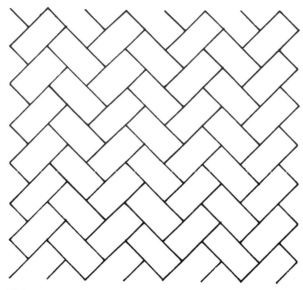

In figure **26.4** the same basket-weave pattern is repeated three times. Notice how coloring emphasizes different aspects of its structure. Figures **26.5** and **26.6** show further elaborations of the basketweave pattern.

26.4a

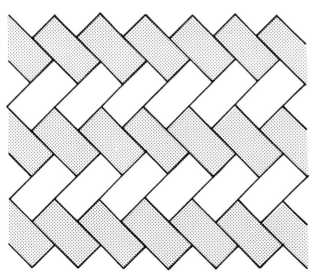

26.4b

26.4c

26.5

Figure 26.6
(a) Congo, Africa
(b) Italy, sixteenth century

26.6a

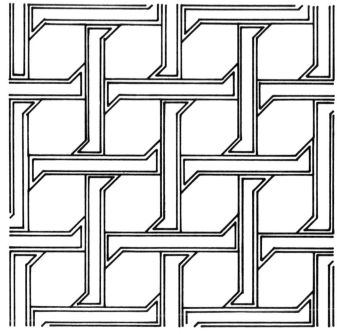

26.6b

26.7a

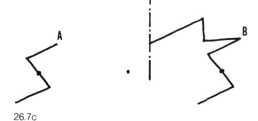

26.7b

Creating Fundamental Regions

How do you develop *p2gg* patterns that contain interlocked packings of fundamental regions? As in figure **26.7** first draw a row of three equally spaced points. Then, as shown in frame (a), draw two identical lines with twofold rotation through the first and third points. (Note in the diagram that the upper ends of these lines are labeled A and B.) The next step, which is outlined in frame (b), is the most critical. It consists of drawing the perpendicular bisector of the line that joins points A and B. Then, as illustrated in frame (c), you can draw any line you choose between point B and the perpendicular bisector. If you then glide-reflect that line, as shown in frame (d), it will connect with point A. After that the going is easy. Simply rotate the figure through a half-turn and add any line with twofold symmetry through the central point. The process yields two fundamental regions like those in frame (f) that under translation and glide reflection produce the *p2gg* outline of birds in figure **26.8**.

26.7c

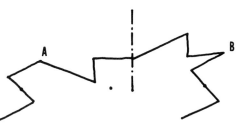

26.7d

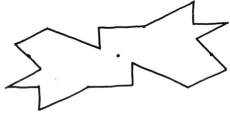

26.7e

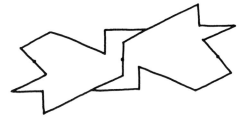

26.7f

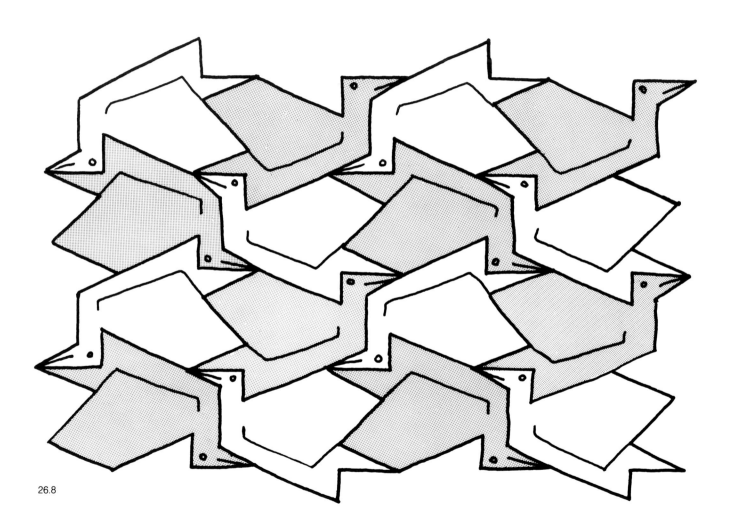

26.8

Figure **26.9** shows a *p2gg* design by M. C. Escher. After analyzing it in accord with the procedure just described, you will discover that each fundamental region contains two fish, as shown in figure **26.10**. Usually the motifs in Escher's designs encompass one or more fundamental regions. Here, however, each motif is only part of a fundamental region.

With a little practice you can also draw fundamental regions that contain more than one motif. As examples you can see how each bird in figure 26.8 can be divided to show two birds as in figure **26.11** or three birds as in figure **26.12**. Obviously, fundamental regions of other symmetry groups can be subdivided in a similar fashion.

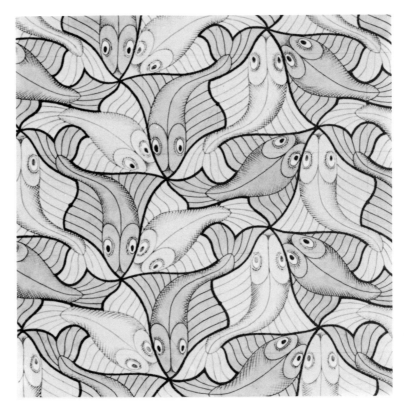

26.9

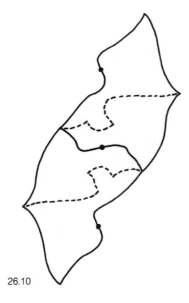

26.10

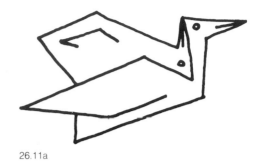

26.11a

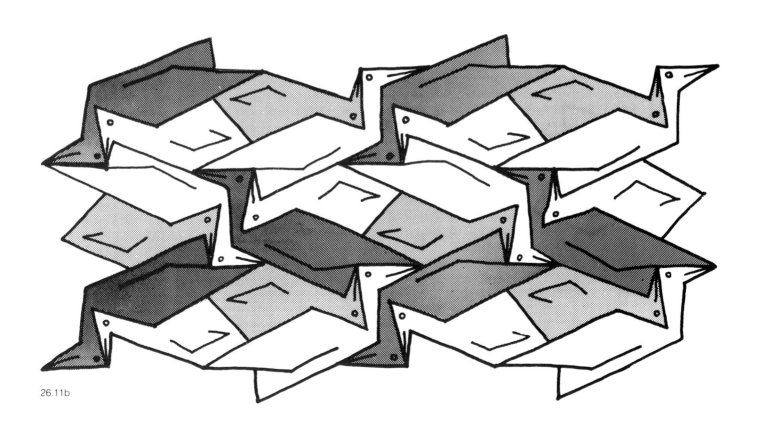

26.11b

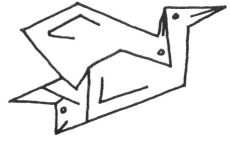

26.12a

26.12b

*Look around you—can you see
space? You only see things.*

Diego Rivera

*In the end it is space itself which
is modularized.*

Lawrence B. Anderson

27
Reflections in Four
Sides of a Rectangle:
Group *p2mm*

The Kaleidoscopic Box

A rectangular enclosure of four mirrors arranged like the sides of a sandbox produces by multiple reflection the *p2mm* pattern. This rectangular kaleidoscope is easy to make by taping four mirrors together. When you surround a single comma with the mirrors, images will reflect from mirror to mirror to form the *p2mm* pattern of figure **27.1**.

Looking at the solid lines of the figure you can see that two different types of mirrors alternate with one another horizontally and two different types alternate with one another vertically. The ovals with their distinguishing marks locate the four different types of 2*mm* centers that occur at the intersections of the mirrors. Four of those centers mark the corners of each mesh or kaleidoscopic box. Whereas the fundamental region that repeats by reflection is identical to one mesh, you can see that the unit cell, which repeats by translation, encompasses four meshes.

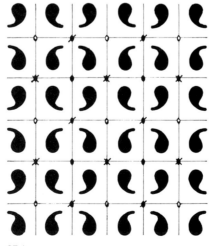

27.1

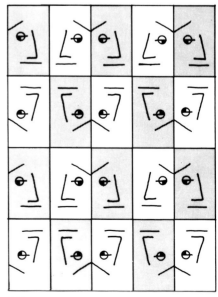

27.2

A Limited Fundamental Region

The only permissible shape for the fundamental region of a *p2mm* group is a rectangle bounded by mirror lines. Figure **27.2** shows features of a face within *p2mm* fundamental regions. If you join images across the mirror lines, that is, if you use images with bilateral symmetry, you can create designs similar to the one produced by M. C. Escher in figure **27.3**. In that design half of each of the four bilateral images fit together to form a rectangle.

27.3

Examples of the Group *p2mm*
More usual in the *p2mm* pattern is the expression of elements with *2mm* symmetry. Figure **27.4** shows examples. You can also stack *t2mm* bands to produce *p2mm* patterns as in figure **27.5**.

Figure 27.4
(a) American Indian, Nez Percé
(b) Romanesque
(c) mosaic pavement, Florence baptistry

27.4a

27.4b

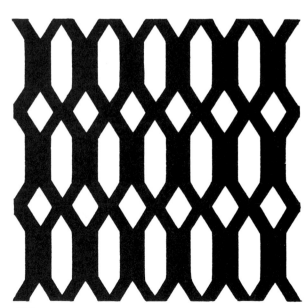

27.4c

Figure 27.5
(a) American Indian, Navaho
(b) ancient Egypt

27.5a

27.5b

See if you can locate the four different rotocenters in each of the brickwork patterns of figure **27.6**.

Figure 27.6
(a), (b), (c) brickwork patterns
(d) Italian, twentieth century design for an open wall
(e) ancient Egyptian, woven mat design
(f) design from the Sandwich Islands

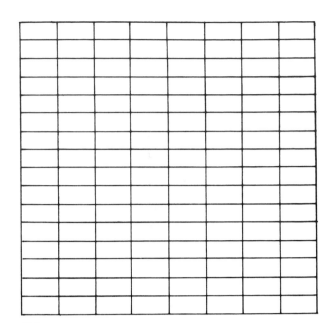

27.6a

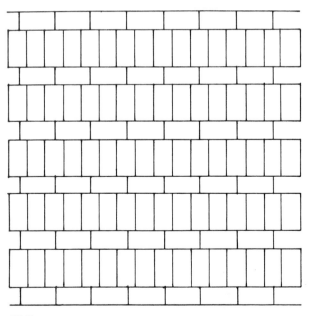

27.6b

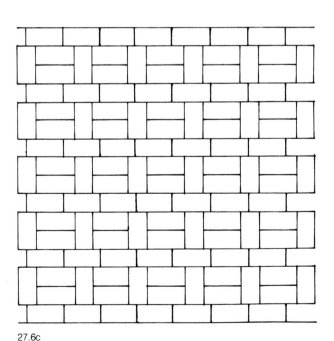

27.6c

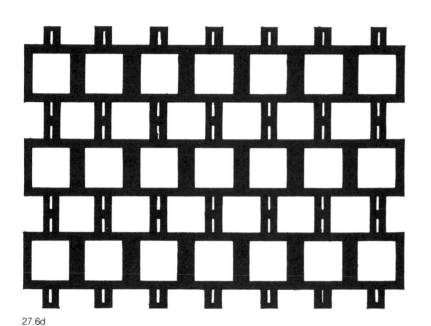

27.6d

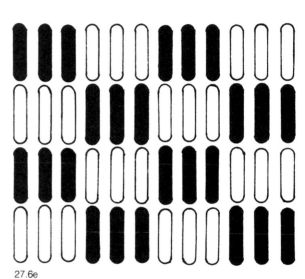

27.6e

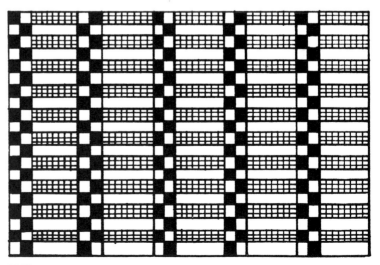

27.6f

Mazes intricate.
Eccentric, interwov'd, yet regular
. . . when most irregular they
seem.

John Milton

28
Perpendicular Mirrors and Perpendicular Glide Reflections: Group c2mm

Shifting Structures

Group c2mm is one of the most interesting of the plane groups. It contains a large number of symmetries. When viewing a c2mm design you sometimes lose sight of a given set of relations and see instead relations of a totally different sort. This shift in perceived structure may be followed by another shift in which you become aware of still other relations. The shifts are sudden and for the most part unconscious. Although in any c2mm design all the structural relations are continuously present, their interrelations are so complex that your mind can seize only a few of them at any one time. By accenting one set or another you can develop patterns quite different in appearance. Sometimes the c2mm pattern will look like a staggered arrangement of 2mm motifs, sometimes like reflected arrangements of simple twofold centers, and sometimes like row upon row of t2mg or t2mm bands. All these arrangements exist simultaneously within the pattern.

Structure of Group c2mm

Before we review differences in emphasis, however, let us examine the underlying structure of the c2mm pattern as revealed by the commas in figure 28.1. Observe in the figure that parallel mirrors and glide lines that alternate with one another run both horizontally and vertically. Where mirror lines intersect perpendicularly you find two distinct types of 2mm centers. Where glide lines intersect perpendicularly, you find two simple twofold centers that are mirror images of one another.

Building Blocks

A single mesh marked by four different twofold centers has the shape of a rhombus and is indicated by the smaller shaded area in frame (b). The unit cell, which is also shaded, has an area of four meshes. Although the unit cell will generate the entire pattern by translation, convention has established a larger generating cell. In frame (c) it is the shaded rectangle with an area of two unit cells. Its corners and center fall on the same 2mm rotocenter. This rectangle gives the group its name, c2mm, the group generated by a centered rectangle, c, whose corners and center fall on 2mm rotocenters.

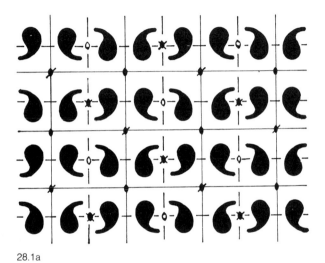

28.1a

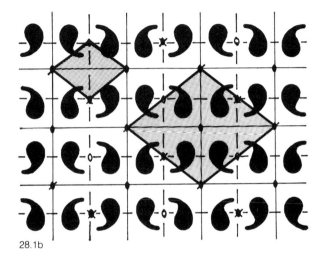

28.1b

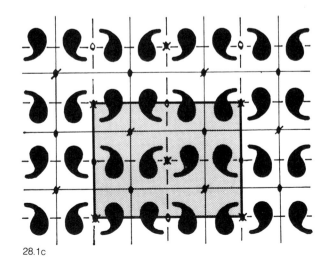

28.1c

Examples of c2mm
The designs in figure **28.2** accent the staggered arrangement of 2mm units. The staggering occurs both vertically and horizontally along lines of glide reflection. The same staggering occurs in figure **28.3** where the 2mm units are lozenge shapes.

In frame (a) of figure **28.4** the 2mm symmetry is less apparent because the accent falls on the S-forms that come in mirrored pairs. Observe how the entire pattern can be generated by reflecting the S-forms in perpendicular mirrors.

Frames (b) and (c) of Figure 28.4 show patterns that emphasize almost equally the 2mm and simple twofold centers. Those designs are the ones that produce the sudden shifts of perceived structure.

Figure 28.2
(a) Iroquois design of interwoven beads
(b) Turkish, sixteenth century

28.2a

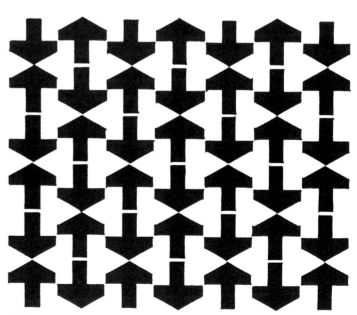

28.2b

Figure 28.3
(a) ancient Greek
(b) medieval pattern
(c) design by Archibald Christie
(d) Pompeian mosaic

28.3c

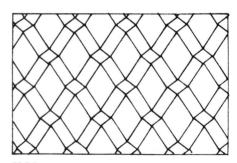

28.3d

28.3a

28.3b

Figure 28.4
(a) Japanese
(b) Italian, sixteenth century
(c) medieval design

28.4a

28.4b

28.4c

In figure **28.5** the S-shaped elements link together to form linear bands with *t2mg* symmetry. You can also see *t2mg* bands in figure **28.6**—but only with effort, since the coloring accents *t2mm* bands.

Figure 28.5
(a) from India
(b) African

Figure 28.6
Arabian

28.5a

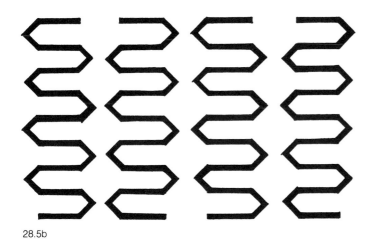

28.5b

28.6

Figure **28.7** shows simple
mosaics and brickwork in the
c2mm arrangement.

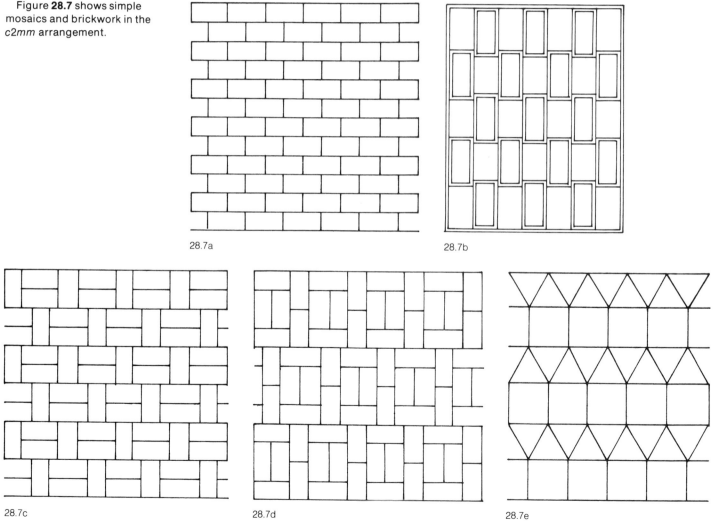

28.7a

28.7b

28.7c

28.7d

28.7e

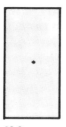
28.8a

28.8b

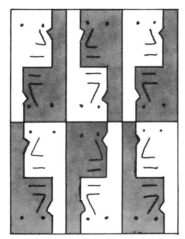
28.8c

Constructing the Fundamental Region

So far no mention has been made of the fundamental region of the *c2mm* pattern. It happens to have an area equal to one mesh—but what shape can it have and how can you construct it easily? Figure **28.8** gives the answers. When you draw a line with twofold symmetry through the center of a rectangle, you obtain two fundamental regions that can be reflected in the four sides of the rectangle to obtain a *c2mm* pattern. The rectangle and line in frames (a) and (b) produce the outlines of the heads in frame (c).

Figure **28.9** shows designs in which two fundamental regions join to form the repetitive motif, and figure **28.10** shows designs based on groups of four fundamental regions.

Figure 28.9
(a) medieval heraldic design, type vair
(b) American patchwork design, c. 1850

28.9a

28.9b

28.10a

Figure 28.10
(a) Chinese
(b), (c) Italian, twentieth century,
ceramic design
(d) Japanese

28.10b

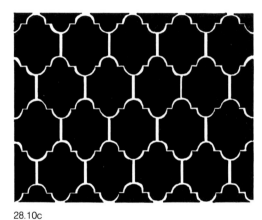

28.10c

28.10d

Exercises

1. Can you stack the *t2mg* band ornament in figure 17.3a to generate both *p2mg* and *c2mm* designs?

2. If you consider only the black portions of figure 27.6e, to what group would you assign the design?

3. Both frames (a) and (c) of figure 25.12 show *p2mg* designs. However, if you consider only the black portions of each design, to what group would you assign them?

4. Answer the same questions for the *p2gg* designs in frames (b) and (c) of figure 26.4.

5. Locate a mesh, a fundamental region, and a unit cell for the *p2gg* design in figure 26.6b.

6. Locate a mesh, a fundamental region, a primitive unit cell *p*, and a centered cell *c*, for the *c2mm* design in figure 28.4a.

7. To what group does the Arabic design in figure **28.11** belong? It will require careful study.

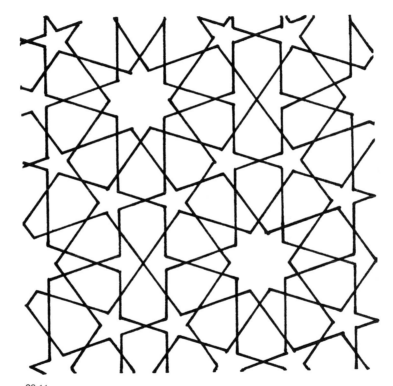

28.11

29
Three Rotations Through 120°: Group *p3*

Having completed a review of the five groups that contain only twofold centers of rotation, let us now examine the three groups with only threefold centers. They are lively groups, full of swirling motion and dynamic interaction. Interestingly enough, they have not enjoyed the popularity of some of the other groups. Perhaps they have been considered too lively.

Group *p3*

In each of the three groups, straight lines pass through three types of threefold centers. Figure **29.1**, for example, illustrates group *p3* which contains rotations without reflections, and you can see that all three rotocenters lie on straight lines. You can also see that each threefold rotocenter of the same type has the same orientation.

The Generating Units

The shadings in figure **29.2** illustrate the different building blocks of the *p3* pattern. The small triangle unites three different rotocenters to depict a single mesh in a triangular net. (Notice that here, for the first time, the net contains meshes of triangles rather than parallelograms.) The large triangle connects three rotocenters of the same type. The small parallelogram shows a fundamental region that will replicate the entire pattern by means of successive rotations of 120°; and the large parallelogram depicts a unit cell that will replicate the pattern through successive translations. Because the shaded hexagon has exactly the same area and contents as the large parallelogram, it too is a unit cell.

Figure **29.3** shows explicitly how hexagonal tiles can generate the *p3* pattern. Each tile is a unit cell. Figure **29.4** shows a similar design but the pattern is not divided into tiles. The outlines of the tiles are also omitted in figure **29.5** but their would-be locations are obvious.

29.1

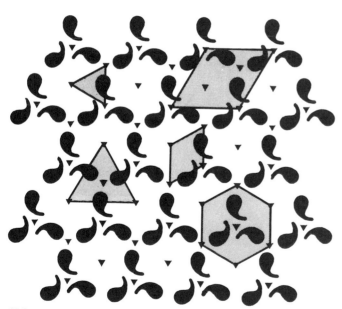

29.2

29.3

29.4

29.5

The designs in figures 29.3–29.6 are Arabian. Can you find the three different threefold centers in Figure **29.6**? (Don't be put off by the six-pointed stars; their sixfold symmetry does not extend throughout the entire pattern.)

Using the Hexagonal Cell
You can put the hexagonal cell to good use when you make *p*3 designs of interlocked fundamental regions. Simply draw any line you wish through the edge of a hexagon. Figure **29.7**a gives an example. When you rotate that line through 120° at each successive corner of the hexagon, you will obtain a closed figure like the one in frame (b). Then, after you add lines with threefold rotation through the center of the figure, as in frame (c), you will obtain three fundamental regions which together translate to produce a continuous *p*3 pattern. Translations of the design in figure 29.7c produce the outlines of the birds in figure **29.8**.

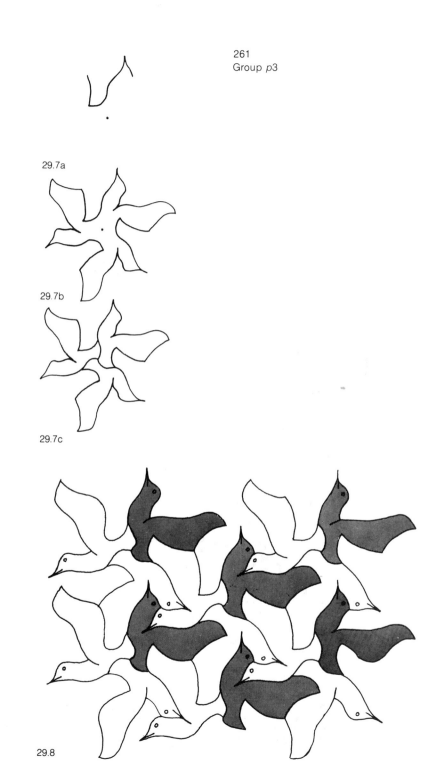

29.7a

29.7b

29.7c

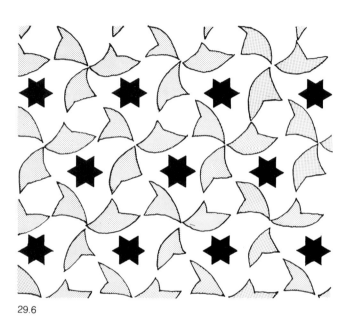

29.6

29.8

Knowing this procedure, you should have little difficulty analyzing the designs of M. C. Escher in figures **29.9** and **29.10**. Simply locate the centers of threefold rotation and isolate a centered hexagon. You will then find one type of line repeated six times around the perimeter of the hexagon and another type of line repeated three times at the center.

Escher may not have used the centered hexagon as a generating unit, of course, since different combinations of operations can produce identical results. Another simple generator of the $p3$ group, for example, is a pair of 120° rotations. If a motif rotates 120° around first one point and then another, again and again, it will spread across the plane to form a $p3$ pattern. You can easily prove this for yourself.

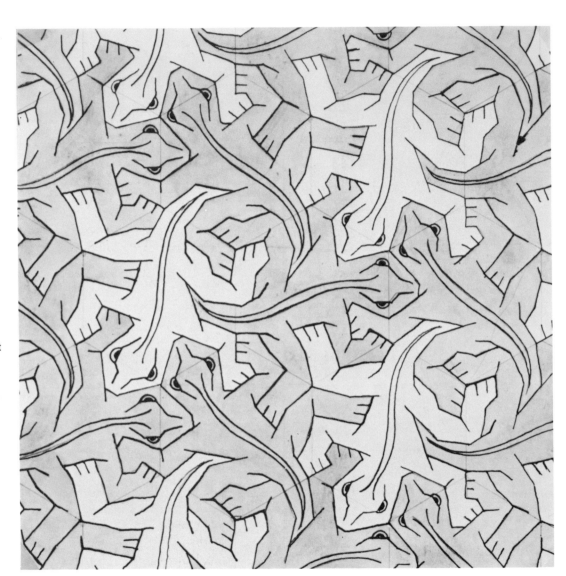

29.9

29.10

30
Reflections in an Equilateral Triangle: Group p3m1

Another Kaleidoscopic Box

Pattern p3m1 combines threefold rotocenters with mirror lines so that a 3m rotocenter marks each intersection of mirrors. Group p3m1 is one of the kaleidoscopic groups because it can be generated by multiple reflections in a box of mirrors—in this case a box of three vertical mirrors that enclose an equilateral triangle.

The p3m1 pattern of commas in figure **30.1** is repeated in figure **30.2** with the addition of shadings that show its structural units. The small shaded triangle which connects three different threefold centers defines the mesh whose edges outline the kaleidoscopic box. If you stand mirrors along these edges, the single comma inside will reflect and re-reflect to produce the entire p3m1 design.

Designations

You may wonder why the group is called p3m1 rather than p3m. After all, the shaded parallelogram shows a primitive cell, p, whose corners fall on 3m centers. The Hermann-Mauguin designation, however, places a 1 in the fourth position to indicate the presence of a mirror along the long diagonal of the unit cell, and a 1 in the third position to indicate the presence of a mirror along the short diagonal of the unit cell. Because you find a mirror along the long diagonal of the parallelogram of figure 30.2 the group is called p3m1.

More Generating Cells

The large shaded triangle in figure 30.2 connects three lattice points to enclose half the area of the unit cell. You can see that the mirrors inside the triangle bisect the angles formed by the lattice lines. (This is in contrast to the mirrors of group p31m which, as described in the next chapter, fall on the lattice lines.)

The shaded hexagon in figure 30.2 shows an alternative unit cell. It has the same area and contents as the parallelogram and also reproduces the entire pattern through translation. As a practical matter, you will find the hexagonal cell easier to use. Simply draw a 3m design in the center of a hexagon and slide the hexagon this way and that to fill the plane.

Figure **30.3**a depicts an obvious use of the hexagonal unit cell. The 3m motif sits with the same orientation in each hexagonal tile. In contrast the hexagons in frames (b) and (c) do not constitute unit cells; they are too small.

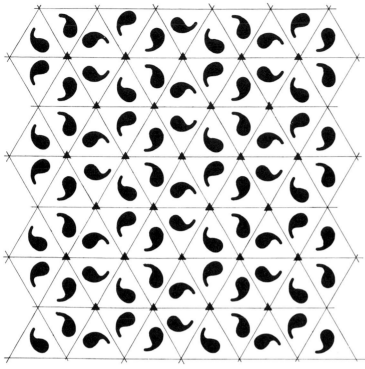

30.1

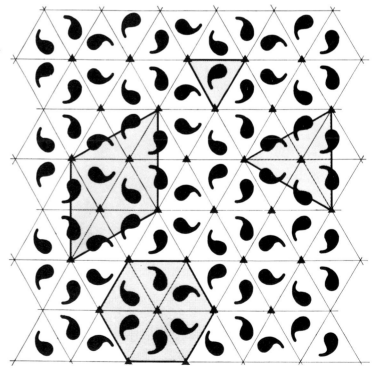

30.2

Figure 30.3
(a) Chinese
(b) Persian
(c) Chinese

30.3a

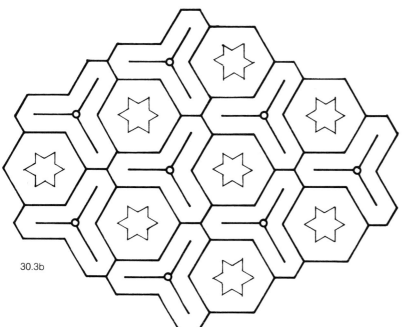

30.3b

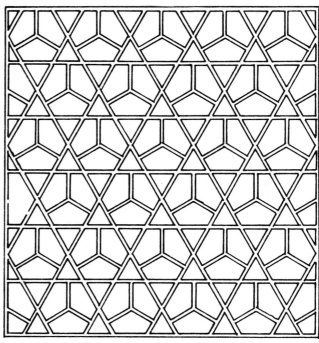

30.3c

Figure **30.4** shows *p*3*m*1 variations on triangular motifs. Their symmetries are obvious.

30.4a

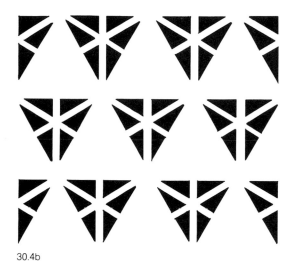

30.4b

30.4c

A Limited Fundamental Region
Since the fundamental region for
p3m1 is the simple equilateral
triangle of the kaleidoscopic box,
you can not make interlocked jigsaw patterns of fundamental regions. Like the faces in figure
30.5, you can set different designs within the pieces, but each
piece remains a triangle. You can,
however, use bilateral images
that cross the mirror lines as
Escher has done in figure **30.6**.
There, each fundamental region
contains half a fish, half a lizard,
and half a bat.

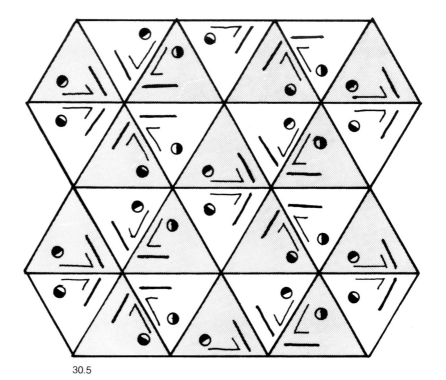

30.5

30.6

31
Reflections of 120° Turns: Group *p31m*

The commas of figure **31.1** illustrate the third group with three threefold centers, group *p31m*. One of the centers lies on intersecting mirrors while the other two are mirror images of one another. That disposition of rotocenters contrasts, of course, with group *p3m1* described in the last chapter, in which all three centers lie on mirrors.

A Comparison

It is instructive to compare figure **31.2**, which shows the building blocks in the *p31m* pattern, with figure 30.2 which shows similar units in the *p3m1* pattern. In both figures a small triangle depicts a mesh that interconnects the three different rotocenters. In *p3m1* the mesh is bounded by three mirrors whereas in *p31m* it is bisected by a single mirror. In both figures the parallelogram shows a unit cell. However, it has a mirror along the long diagonal in *p3m1* and a mirror along the short diagonal in *p31m*. The large triangles that connect three lattice points of the same type contain mirrors that bisect the angles formed by the lattice lines in *p3m1* and mirrors that fall on the lattice lines in *p31m*. The hexagonal unit cells show more distinguishing features: they contain the same *3m* motif, but with different orientations. In the *p3m1* group of figure 30.2 the mirrors bisect the angles at the corners of the hexagonal cell, whereas in the *p31m* group of figure 31.2 the mirrors bisect the edges of the cell. A simple procedure for generating the two groups is therefore obvious. Simply draw a *3m* motif within a hexagon. If the mirrors through the motif intersect the corners of the hexagon, you can generate a *p3m1* pattern. If instead, the mirrors intersect the edges, you can generate a *p31m* pattern.

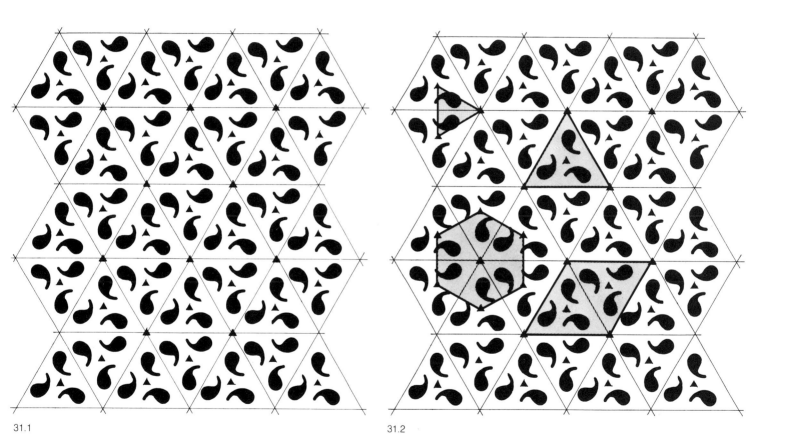

31.1

31.2

31.3a

Examples of *p*31*m*

The Japanese design in Figure **31.3**a makes use of a 3*m* motif, an irregular hexagon, that appears to interweave with itself. The regular hexagon that constitutes the unit cell can be found by connecting the centers of the six interstices around the 3*m* motif. You can see that the interstices occur in mirrored pairs. Frame (b) shows a similar design from China that contains opposite-handed vacancies between large equilateral triangles.

Figure **31.4** illustrates several different treatments of essentially the same 3*m* motif. In each example the motifs join three at a time to form opposite-handed threefold rotocenters.

31.3b

Figure 31.4
(a) Chinese
(b) Chinese
(c) Russian

31.4a

31.4b

31.4c

31.5a

Use of the Kaleidoscopic Box
Figure **31.5** shows more variations on a theme. However, instead of analyzing them in terms of the hexagonal unit cell, let's examine them from the point of view of the kaleidoscopic box that we used for $p3m1$ patterns. Frame (a) shows the procedure. When a motif that has simple threefold symmetry is reflected in the three sides of an equilateral triangle, a $p31m$ pattern comes into existence. In frame (a) the three-armed swastika on each regular triangular tile participates in the $p31m$ design by surrounding itself on all three sides with its own reflected image. You thus have two practical methods to generate $p31m$ designs: translate a regular hexagonal cell that contains a $3m$ motif located so that its mirrors bisect the edges of the cell, or reflect an equilateral triangle that contains a motif with simple threefold rotation.

Figure 31.5
(a) Persian, thirteenth century
(b) Arabian
(c) Arabian
(d) Chinese porcelain design

31.5b

31.5c

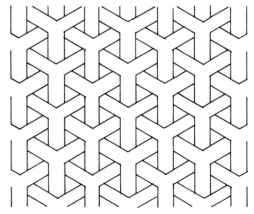

31.5d

The second method is similar to the procedure that produces p3m1 designs. If the equilateral triangle that you reflect contains an asymmetric motif you obtain a p3m1 pattern; if it contains a threefold rotocenter without mirrors you get a p31m pattern.

The Arabian pattern in figure **31.6** presents a good opportunity to analyze a p31m pattern in terms of both its hexagonal unit cell and its kaleidoscopic triangular cell. If you connect six simple threefold centers you get the hexagonal cell; if you connect three 3m centers you get the kaleidoscopic cell.

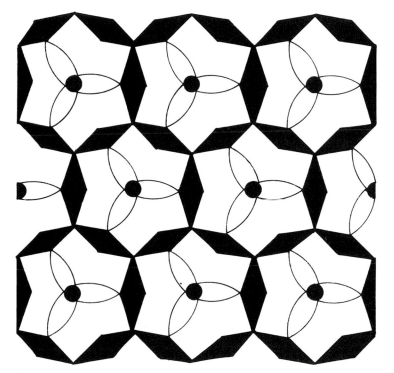

31.6

Two Groups

The reason for focusing on the differences between the $p31m$ and $p3m1$ groups is to clarify their differentiation but also, more important, to illustrate the curious complexity that arises from the interaction of simple operations. The $p31m$ and $p3m1$ groups contain exactly the same elements—threefold rotations and mirror lines. And yet those elements combine to form two distinctly different groups. Regular designs with reflections and threefold centers fall inevitably into either one group or the other.

The Fundamental Region

Figure **31.7** shows how to make $p31m$ designs of interlocked fundamental regions. Simply repeat under threefold rotation any line drawn from the center of an equilateral triangle to its periphery. This procedure yields three interlocked fundamental regions. The other regions arise through kaleidoscopic reflections. You can also ignore the mirror lines by grouping two fundamental regions to form bilaterally symmetric images as M. C. Escher did in the design of figure **31.8**.

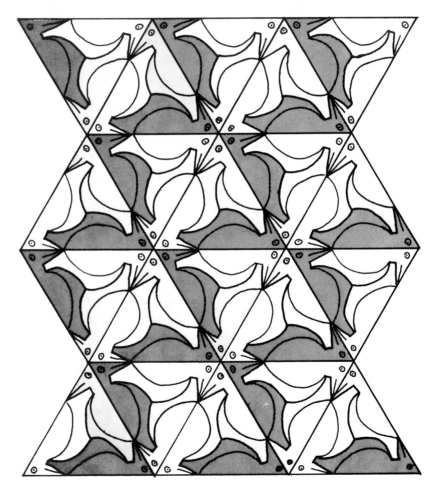

31.7

31.8

Exercises

1. In figure 29.3 the hexagonal unit cell is obvious. Can you also locate a parallelogram that is a unit cell?

2. In figure 29.5, which depicts a p3 pattern, locate a mesh, a fundamental region, a parallelogram that is a unit cell, and a hexagonal unit cell.

3. Use the triskelion in figure 7.2b to generate both a p3 and a p31m design.

4. Use the 3m design of the green pepper in figure 7.8 to generate both p3m1 and p31m designs.

5. Although present, no mention was made of glide lines in the p3m1 and p31m patterns. See if you can sketch their locations in figures 30.1 and 31.1. If you locate them correctly they will have the same relation to the intersecting mirror lines in both figures.

32
Quarter-Turns:
Group *p4*

As indicated in figure 20.1, three plane groups contain fourfold rotocenters: groups *p4*, *p4mm*, and *p4gm*. Each of these groups contains two types of fourfold centers as well as one type of twofold center. Every fourfold center of the same type has the same orientation. The twofold centers have two different orientations.

Group *p4*

The commas in figure **32.1** illustrate the *p4* arrangement in which the four- and twofold centers alternate along perpendicular lines. The small shaded square in frame (b) depicts a single mesh within the net of interconnected centers. The mesh also describes the fundamental region that generates the entire pattern through half-turns and quarter-turns. The large shaded square shows a unit cell that generates the pattern through translation. The group is designated *p4* because the unit cell contains only one fourfold lattice point of the type shared by its corners.

Examples of *p4*

The swirling arrows in figure **32.2** from an advertisement of Spencer Industrial Vacuum Systems show clearly an example of the *p4* group. So do the parallelograms in figure **32.3**. You can see that the twofold symmetry of the parallelograms has two different orientations. The Chinese designs in figure **32.4** are more complicated, but in each one you will find twofold centers on the perpendicular bisectors between adjacent fourfold centers so that the three different centers taken together mark the corners of a 45°-45°-90° triangle. Notice the similarities among frames (b) and (c) of figure 32.4 and the designs from ancient Egypt in figure **32.5**. The interlaced designs of figure **32.6** are more complex.

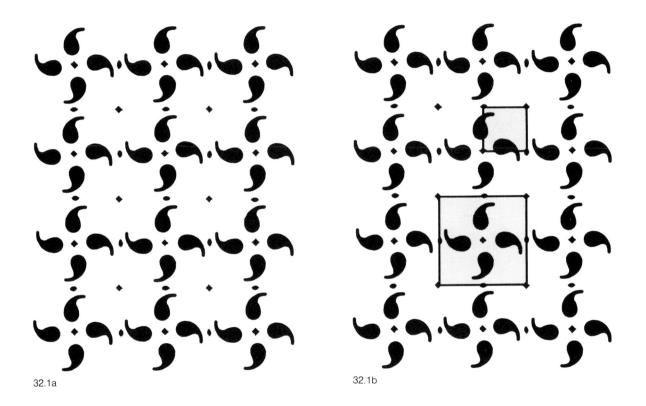

32.1a

32.1b

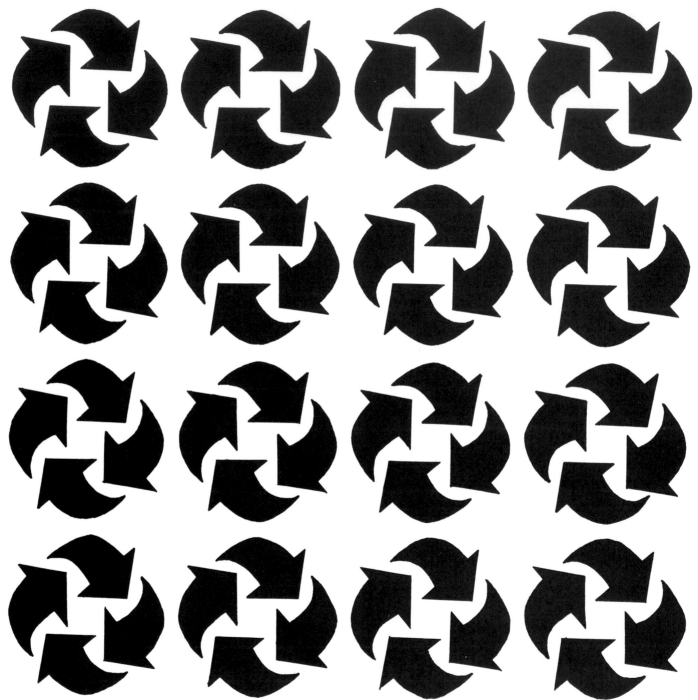

32.2

32.3

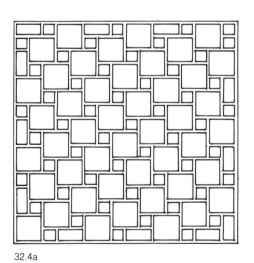

32.4a

32.4b

32.4c

32.5a

32.5b

Figure 32.6
(a) Chinese lattice design
(b) Chinese lattice design
(c) design from Ethiopia
(d) French Romanesque
(e) redrawn from Archibald
Christie [29: p. 284]
(f) Arabic

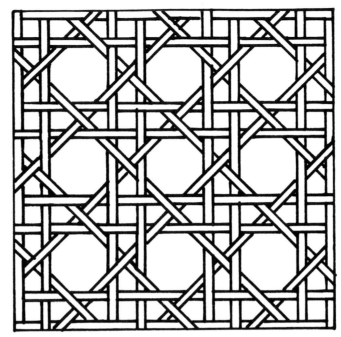

32.6a

32.6b

32.6c

32.6d

32.6e

32.6f

Figure **32.7** is an architectural
example of the *p*4 group. It is a
plan, redrawn from Le Corbusier,
of a proposed city, LaVille
Radieuse, in which each city
block has group-4 symmetry and
each apartment tower has 4*mm*
symmetry.

32.7

32.8a

32.8b

Fundamental Regions

Figure **32.8** illustrates the trick of
drawing interlocked fundamental
regions in the *p*4 arrangement.
Rotate any line of your choosing
through half-turns at one end and
quarter-turns at the other to obtain a *p*4 enclosure of lines. As an
example, the line element in
frame (a) joins with itself after a
half-turn in frame (b) and makes a
complete enclosure in frame (c).
The addition of a fourfold rotocenter at the center of the enclosure produces four interlocked
fundamental regions which cover
the plane under translation.
Frame (e) shows refinements of
the outlines in frame (d). Each
animal is a fundamental region.

If, in accord with this procedure, you analyze the *p*4 design of
M. C. Escher in figure **32.9**, you
will see that he drew four lines directly from the central rotocenter
within the enclosure to the
twofold centers on each edge.
This is permissible in a *p*4 design
but not necessary, since lines
from the central rotocenter can
meet the perimeter of the enclosure at any point—not necessarily at the twofold centers.

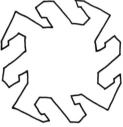

32.8c

32.8d

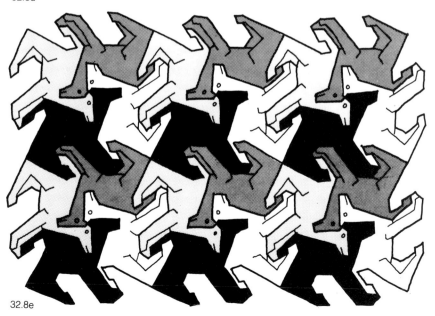

32.8e

32.9

Exercises

1. Locate a mesh, a fundamental region, and a unit cell in the *p*4 design of figure 32.6b.

2. Find the same generating units for Escher's design in figure 32.9.

3. Generate a *p*4 design using the group-4 motif of figure 8.2j.

4. Generate a *p*4 design based on the group-2 motif of hands in figure 6.3b. Remember to give each pair of hands two different orientations.

5. Determine the group designation of the Japanese design in figure **32.10**.

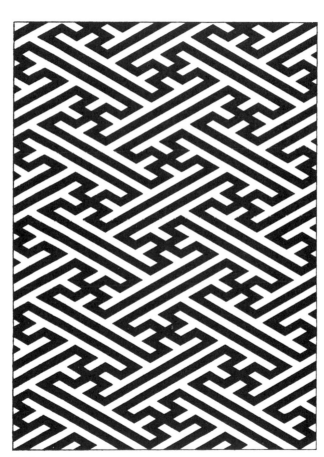

32.10

*And when that comes about that
has not yet been heard, will we be
able to say more or less than we
can now about the unit and its
relationship to the whole?*

John Cage

33
Reflections of
Quarter-Turns:
Group *p4gm*

Group *p4gm*

In group *p4gm* the fourfold centers come in mirror-reflected pairs. The pairing arises because mirror lines run directly through the twofold centers as shown in figure **33.1**. The fourfold centers are reflections of one another, and the 2*mm* centers lie on perpendicular mirrors. The 45°-45°-90° shaded triangle on the left in frame (b) connects the three different types of rotocenters to outline a mesh. The triangle on the right with the same area outlines a fundamental region. Quarter-turns, around the 90° corner of that triangle and reflections across the hypotenuse generate the entire pattern. Eight fundamental regions combine to make the unit cell, shown by shading.

Examples of *p4gm*

Figure **33.2** illustrates a *p4gm* Arabian design that emphasizes about equally the fourfold and twofold centers. You can see that the four-armed motifs are reflections of one another and that the twofold centers, although identical in shape, have two different orientations.

The designs in figure **33.3** emphasize instead the twofold centers. In each example four 2*mm* motifs join to make four-way intersections. These designs combine formality and variety in an especially pleasing manner.

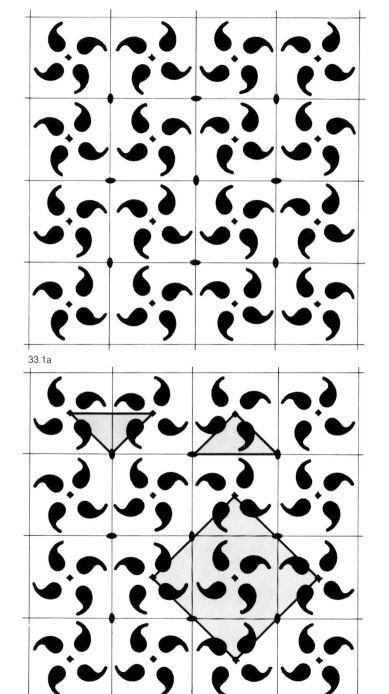

33.1a

33.1b

33.2

Figure 33.3
(a) Arabian
(b) ancient Egyptian
(c) ancient Roman
(d) Chinese lattice design
(e) Chinese lattice design
(f) ancient Egyptian
(g) Chinese porcelain design

33.3a

33.3b

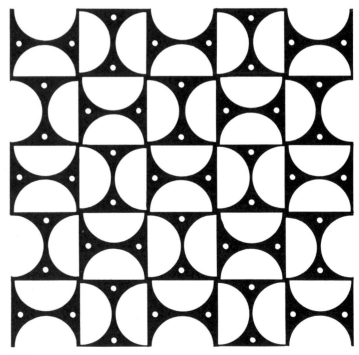

33.3c

33.3d

33.3e

33.3f

33.3g

Figure **33.4** shows basketweave variations of the *p4gm* pattern and figure **33.5** shows how the pattern can be built from regular tiles. Figure **33.6** shows examples of bilateral motifs. (Frame (c) of figure 33.6 is the design we first examined in figure 2.9.)

Figure 33.4
(a) ancient Egyptian
(b) design of the Bakuba tribe, Congo, Africa
(c) Chinese porcelain design
(d) Chinese lattice design

33.4a

33.4b

33.4c

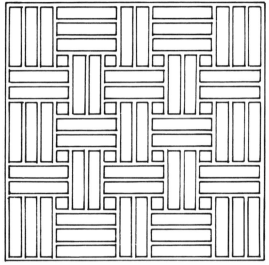

33.4d

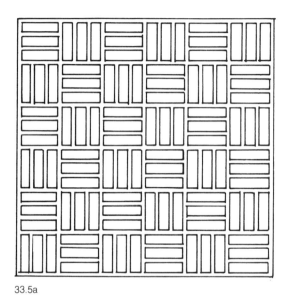

33.5a

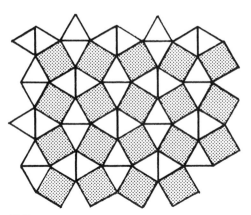

33.5b

Figure 33.6
(a) mother-of-pearl inlay motif,
Turkey
(b) Arabian
(c) Arabian

33.6a

33.6b

33.6c

33.7a

Creating Fundamental Regions
None of these designs picture
motifs that are equivalent to fundamental regions. To construct
individual fundamental regions of
different shapes, draw any line
from the center of a square to the
perimeter and then repeat the line
after a 90° turn. Figure **33.7** shows
the procedure. Frame (b) shows
the fundamental region which results from repetition of the line in
frame (a). Additional repetitions
of that same line fill the square
with four fundamental regions,
and reflections of those regions
generate the entire *p4gm* pattern.
Thus the single line in frame (a)
generates the outlines of the re-
clining dogs in frame (c). Notice
that the corners of the squares
mark the locations of twofold
rotocenters.

This procedure should enable
you to analyze M. C. Escher's
p4gm design in figure **33.8**. When
you connect the twofold centers
at the toes of the angels to outline
a square, you find at its center
an intersection of wings. Consequently each angel as well as
each devil contains two fundamental regions.

33.7b

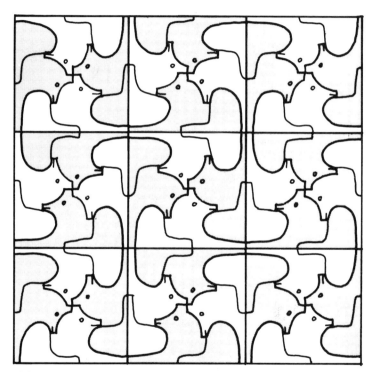

33.7c

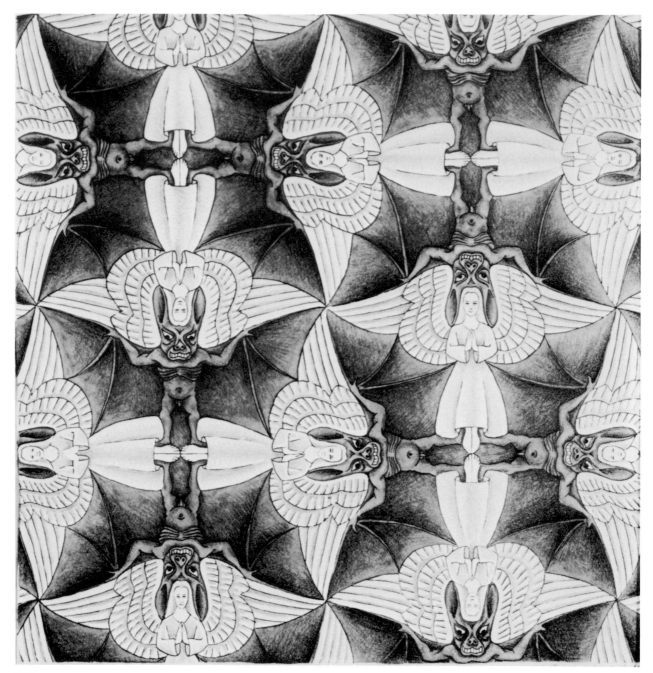

33.8

Exercises

1. Locate a mesh, a fundamental region, and a unit cell in the *p4gm* pattern of figure 33.5b.

2. Locate the same building blocks for Escher's design in figure 33.8.

3. Generate a *p4gm* design using the group-4 motif of figure 8.3c. (Remember to reflect the motif.)

4. Generate a *p4gm* design using the 2*mm* motif of figure 6.14a.

5. See if you can locate all the glide lines in figure 33.1a. (Two intersect at every fourfold center and three intersect at every point midway between twofold and fourfold centers.)

For some minutes Alice stood
without speaking, looking out in
all directions over the country . . .
"I declare it's marked out like a
large chessboard all over the
world—if this is the world at all."

Lewis Carroll

34
Reflections in the Sides
of a 45°-45°-90° Triangle:
Group *p4mm*

A Kaleidoscope

Group *p4mm* is another of the kaleidoscopic groups. It can be generated by an assembly of three mirrors taped together to enclose a 45°-45°-90° triangle. If you stand the mirrors along the perimeter of the shaded triangle in figure **34.1**a you will see within them the entire *p4mm* pattern. As well as picturing the kaleidoscopic cell, the shaded triangle depicts a mesh because it interconnects the three different rotocenters within the pattern— two fourfold centers and a single twofold center. Both fourfolds have 4*mm* symmetry because they fall on four intersecting mirrors; the twofold center with its two different orientations has 2*mm* symmetry because it falls on two intersecting mirrors. The shaded square in frame (b) encloses eight meshes and illustrates the unit cell which generates the pattern through translation.

The Square Grid

The simplest expression of *p4mm* is the square grid that Alice saw in Wonderland and that we see frequently in the everyday landscape. Not everyone likes the square grid. It has come to epitomize man's subjugation of nature. In satellite photographs of the earth, for example, the grid inevitably signals the presence of urban concentrations. Some have referred to the grid as the eczema of the planet. We find it everywhere—in city planning, building facades, wire fences, plaid fabrics, and chessboards. What explains its ubiquitous presence? Simplicity and equality.

The grid is simple because at every intersection two and only two lines cross and neither line deflects the other. Equality arises because the lines cross with impartiality, that is to say, as symmetrically as possible. Their crossing leaves four squares of equal size, and each square contains four right angles—exactly like the crossing itself. In terms of symmetry, each square and each intersection relates to the others through translation, rotation, reflection, and glide reflection. Consequently in the *p4mm* grid, all symmetry operations come into play in an especially straightforward manner.

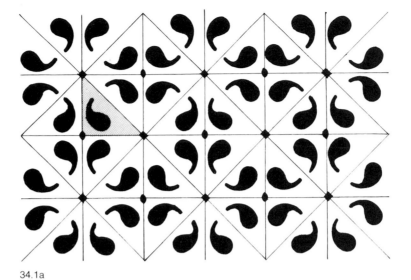

34.1a

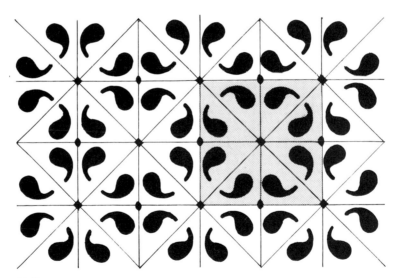

34.1b

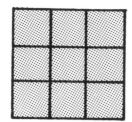

34.2a

Examples of *p4mm*

Figure **34.2** shows two *p4mm* tilings—the square grid and also the common pattern of squares and hexagons. The tiling, after Altair, in figure **34.3** is not so common. It contains squares and pentagons (shown solid) as well as hexagons, seven-sided figures, and octagons. Because only the neighborhoods around the octagons and squares exhibit rotational symmetry, the octagons and squares fix the location of *4mm* rotocenters. The *2mm* centers lie between adjacent hexagons.

The motif of a cross with *4mm* symmetry appears in each of the Moorish designs in figure **34.4**. In frame (c) this cross is swamped by the octagonal stars but it is still apparent and marks the location of a *4mm* center.

Figures **34.5** and **34.6** show *p4mm* designs using circles and squares. Figures **34.7** and **34.8** show Chinese and Arabian designs.

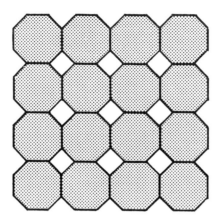

34.2b

34.3

34.4a

34.4b

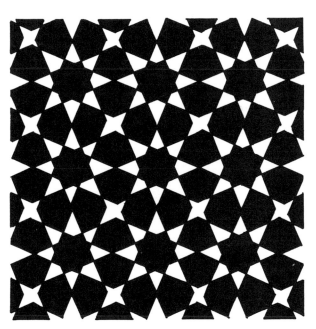

34.4c

Figure 34.5
(a) paving tiles, French, fourteenth century
(b) design inlaid in marble, Italian,
fourteenth century
(c) mosaic, ancient Rome
(d) medieval design

34.5a

34.5b

34.5c

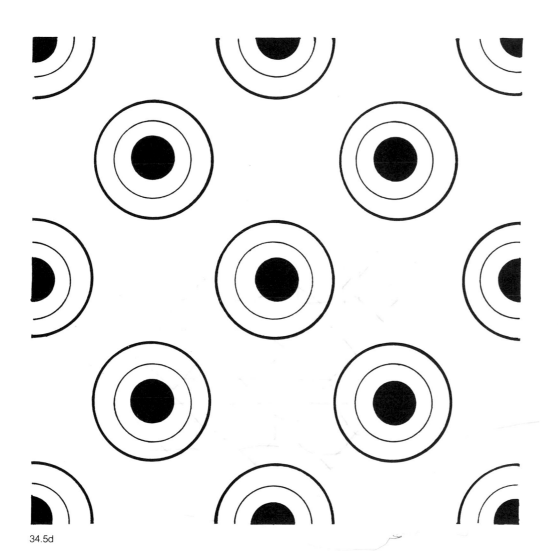

34.5d

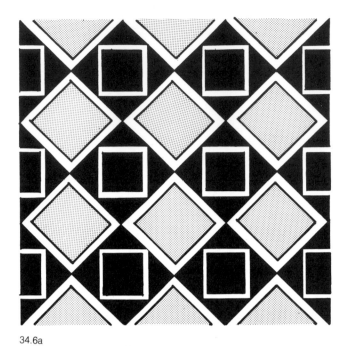

34.6a

Figure 34.6
(a) Byzantine design
(b) tartan pattern
(c) Mayan motif, Uxmal, Yucatan
(d) Japanese
(e) ancient Roman

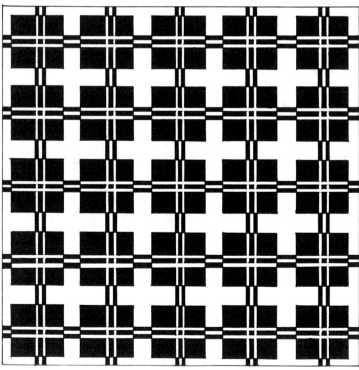

34.6b

34.6c

34.6d

34.6e

34.7a

34.7b

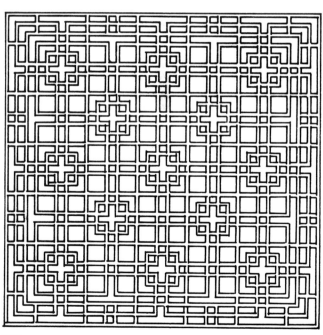

34.7c

34.8a

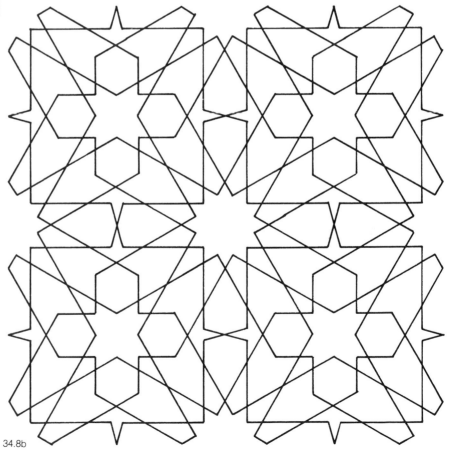

34.8b

34.8c

The Fundamental Region
The mirrors, of course, limit the shape of the fundamental region to a 45°-45°-90° triangle. You can decorate it with features as in figure **34.9** but its shape will remain the same. What happens if in the attempt to obtain bilateral motifs you unite fundamental regions two at a time across the mirrors? You will get still another *p4mm* pattern of squares! You can easily prove this for yourself.

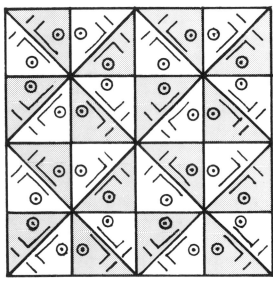

34.9

34.10

Exercises

1. Use the 2*mm* motif of figure 6.14a to generate a *p4mm* design.

2. What is the fundamental region and the unit cell in figure 34.3?

3. If you stack each line group with itself, what plane groups can you generate from figures 17.7d, 18.6d, 18.7b and 18.7d?

4. Name the group designation of the design from India in figure **34.10**.

5. See if you can locate glide lines in figure 34.1. (They pass through twofold centers in perpendicular pairs.)

When Coleridge tried to define beauty, he returned always to one deep thought; beauty, he said, is unity in variety!

Jacob Bronowski

35
Six-Fold Rotations: Group *p*6

We have explored plane groups with four rotocenters and will prove in the appendix that no plane groups exist with fivefold centers. Here let us examine the two groups that contain sixfold rotations. In both, the sixfold centers combine with three- and twofold centers. The sixfold centers always have the same orientation, the threefolds have two different orientations, and the twofolds have three different orientations.

Group *p*6

The group with sixfold centers without mirrors is called *p*6 and is shown by commas in figure **35.1**. The shaded 30°-60°-90° triangle depicts a mesh within the net of rotocenters. It connects the three different centers of rotation.

The shaded parallelogram depicts the primitive unit cell whose corners fall on sixfold centers. Instead of using the parallelogram to generate *p*6 patterns, however, you will likely find it easier to translate the shaded hexagonal cell that has a sixfold rotocenter. Notice that both the parallelogram and the hexagon contain twelve meshes.

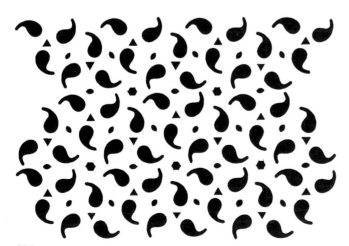

35.1a

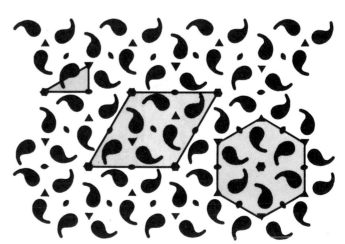

35.1b

Examples of *p*6

Figure **35.2** shows Chinese window designs in the *p*6 arrangement. The sixfold centers fall within hexagons, the threefold centers fall within triangles, and the twofold centers fall between triangles. Figure **35.3** shows a similar arrangement made with regular tiles whose edges all have the same length. The Arabic designs in figure **35.4** are again similar but less regular.

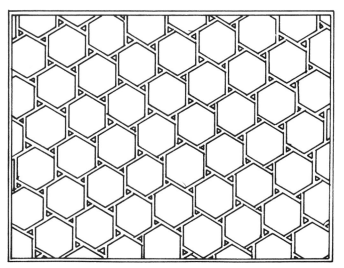

35.2a

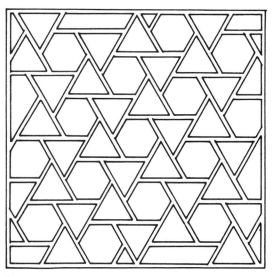

35.2b

35.2c

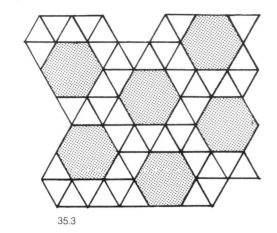

35.3

35.4b

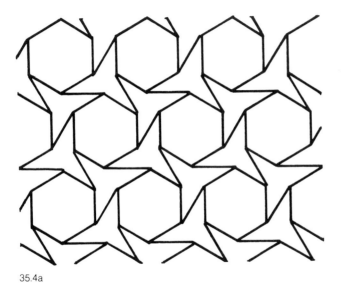

35.4a

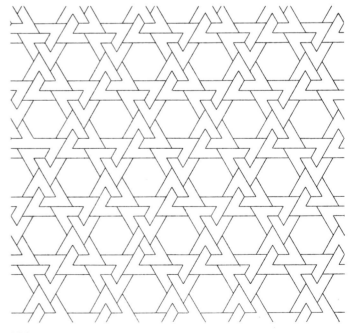

35.4c

35.4d

The twofold motifs in the Arabic patterns in figure **35.5** produce *p*6 patterns with quite a different effect. Notice that the 2*mm* motifs have three different orientations.

Figure **35.6** shows *p*6 interlacements. Frame (a) is a Persian design from the sixteenth century, and frame (b) is developed from a sketch by Leonardo da Vinci. The Arabic design in figure **35.7** shows a complicated interlocked pattern of gears with sixfold symmetry, with each gear containing six fundamental regions. In the Arabic design of figure **35.8**, however, each "gear" contains only three fundamental regions.

35.5a

35.5b

35.6a

35.6b

35.7

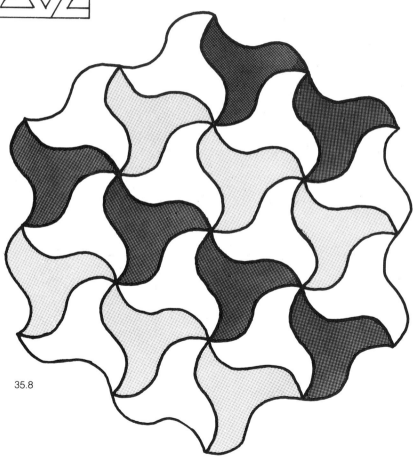

35.8

35.9a

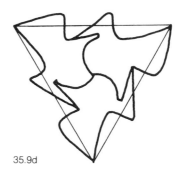

35.9c

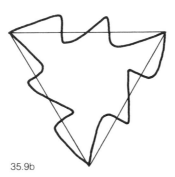

35.9b

35.9d

The Fundamental Region

To draw *p*6 designs in which each piece is a fundamental region, you need only follow the procedure outlined in figure **35.9**. Start with any line such as the curve that crosses the straight line in frame (a). Add a line obtained by rotating the original curve through a half turn, as in frame (b), and repeat the result twice again to make a triangular enclosure as in frame (c). After you add three lines that emanate from a central threefold rotocenter, you obtain three fundamental regions like those shown in frame (d) which outline the birds in frame (e).

35.9e

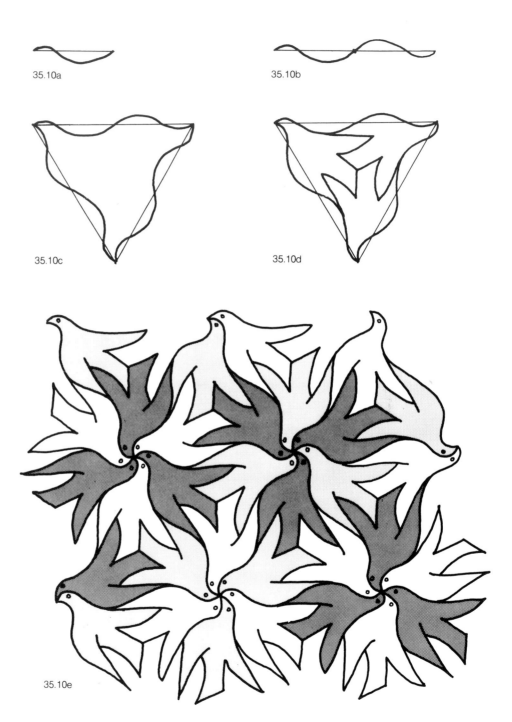

35.10a

35.10b

35.10c

35.10d

Figure **35.10** illustrates again exactly the same procedure so that the line segment in frame (a) produces the outlines of birds in frame (e).

Figure **35.11** shows the procedure applied to M. C. Escher's p6 pattern in figure **35.12**. Notice however, in frame (a), that Escher chose a line segment which, when joined with itself after a twofold rotation, made contact with the central threefold rotocenter. This produced a pattern with a high degree of regularity and alleviated the need to add additional lines from the threefold center.

35.10e

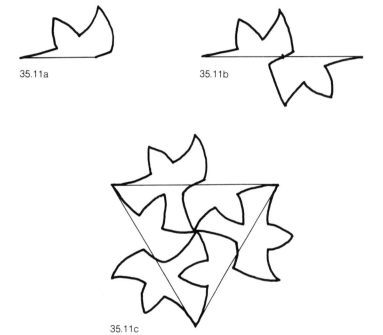

35.11a

35.11b

35.11c

35.12

36
Reflections in the Sides of a 30°-60°-90° Triangle: Group p6mm

A Kaleidoscopic Box

The seventeenth and final plane group is *p6mm*, a straightforward kaleidoscopic group. If you set three mirrors on edge to enclose the 30°-60°-90° shaded triangle in figure **36.1**, the comma inside will reflect from mirror to mirror to produce the entire *p6mm* pattern. The triangle thus depicts a fundamental region. The triangle also depicts a mesh, of course, because it connects the three different rotocenters.

In figure **36.2** the shaded parallelogram composed of twelve meshes defines a unit cell as does the shaded hexagon in figure **36.3**, which contains exactly the same area. Both cells generate the pattern through translation.

Regular Packings

The photograph in figure **36.4** shows a *p6* pattern of close-packed spheres. The centers of the spheres mark points of sixfold symmetry. The centers of the interstices between three spheres have threefold symmetry, and the points of tangency between adjacent spheres have twofold symmetry.

Figure **36.5** shows more examples of regular packings. Each design is a *p6mm* packing of regular tiles.

Figures 36.6–36.8 show still more *p6mm* designs. Frame (a) of figure **36.6** depicts an ancient design from the palace at Nimrud, Mesopotamia, and frame (b) shows a Japanese design. The ornaments in figure **36.7** are Chinese, and those in figure **36.8** are Arabic.

36.1

36.2

36.3

36.4

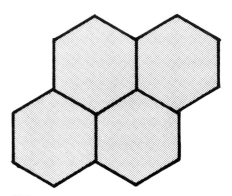

36.5a

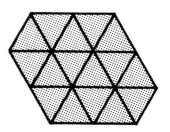

36.5b

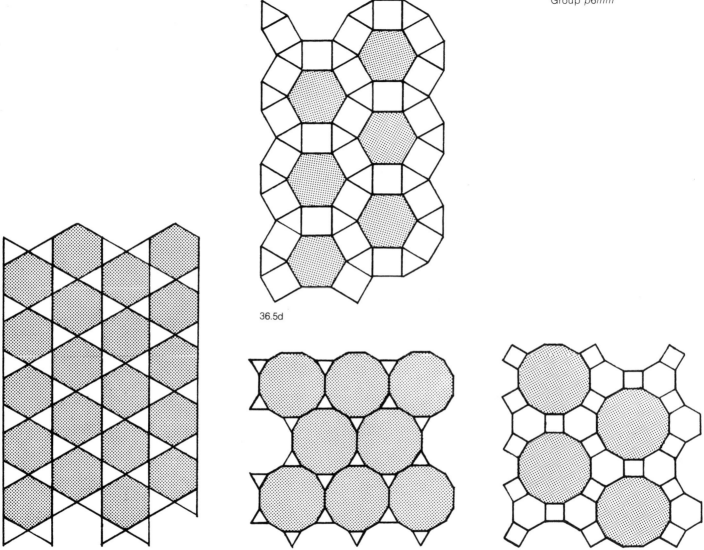

36.5d

36.5c

36.5e

36.5f

36.6b

36.6a

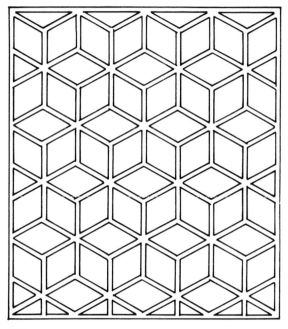

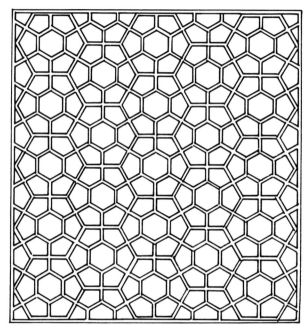

36.7a

36.7b

36.8a

36.8b

36.8c

The Fundamental Region

The mirrors in the *p6mm* pattern prohibit the development of interlocked fundamental regions. As shown in figure **36.9**, each region must have the shape of a 30°-60°-90° triangle.

Exercises

1. Locate the parallelogram and the hexagon that serve as unit cells in the designs of figures 35.3 and 36.8a.

2. If you stack each line group with itself, what plane groups can you generate from figures 18.8a and 18.8b? (Trim the edges of the bands.)

3. Generate a *p6* pattern using the group-2 snake motif of figure 6.5a.

4. Generate a *p6mm* pattern using the 3*m* pepper motif of figure 7.8.

5. See if you can locate the glide lines in figure 36.1. You should find four glides through each twofold center.

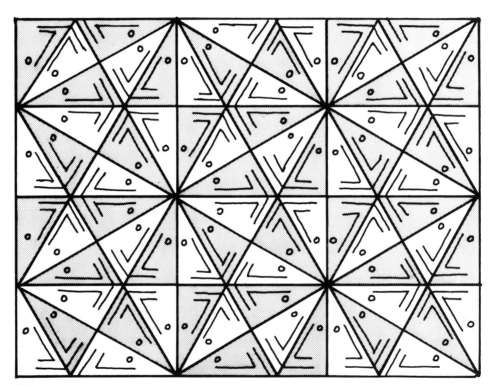

36.9

*All things began in order, so shall
they end, and so shall they begin
again; according to the ordainer
of order and mystical mathematics of the city of heaven.*

Sir Thomas Browne

37
Summary

When we combine the four operations that generate repetition—
translation, rotation, reflection,
and glide reflection—we obtain a
limited number of structural patterns or symmetry groups. Seven
of these patterns form linear
bands and seventeen cover a
plane. For easy reference, all the
configurations of commas that
have been used to illustrate the
groups are repeated in figure **37.1**
along with their group designations.

Also for reference, figure **37.2**
repeats for the seventeen plane
groups all the illustrations of
fundamental regions.

Despite Constraints
Finally, to illustrate the ease with
which designs can be generated,
figure **37.3** shows a wealth of
combinations obtained from a
single line element and its mirror
image. In all these designs no
other elements are used, just the
one line and its reflection. Furthermore, the line and its reflection are joined only end-to-end.
Despite these constraints, an as-
tonishing variety of designs can
be developed. This is the fruit of
symmetry theory.

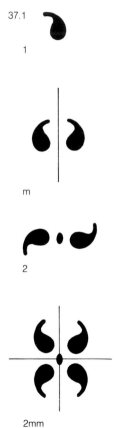

37.1

1

m

2

2mm

3

3m

4

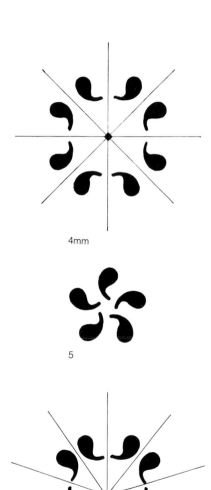

4mm

5

5m

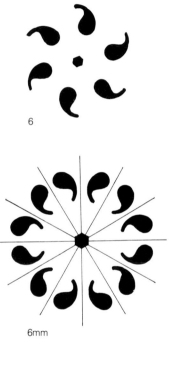

6

6mm

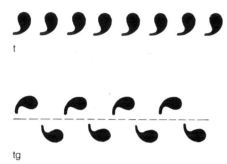

t

tg

tm

mt

t2

t2mg

t2mm

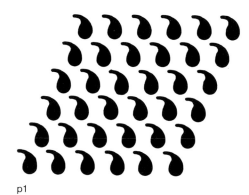

p1

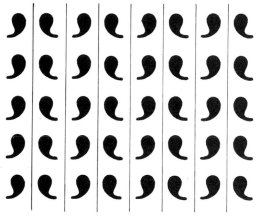

pm

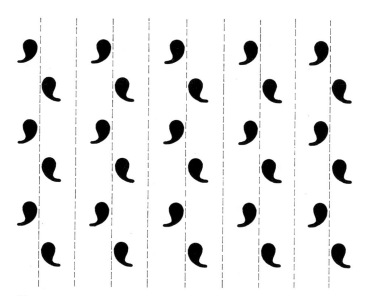

pg

cm

p2

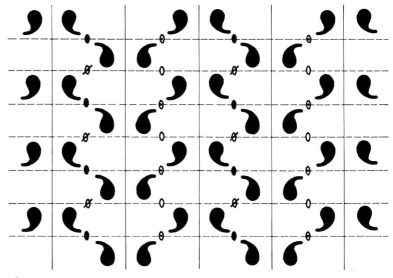

p2mg

p2gg

p2mm

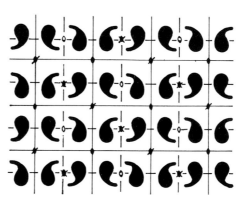

c2mm

p3

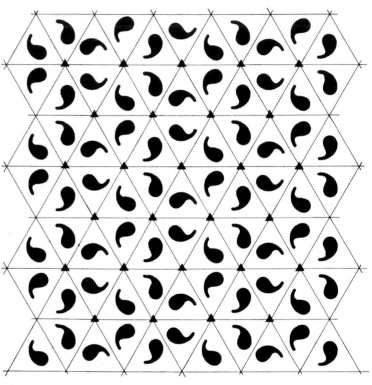

p3m1

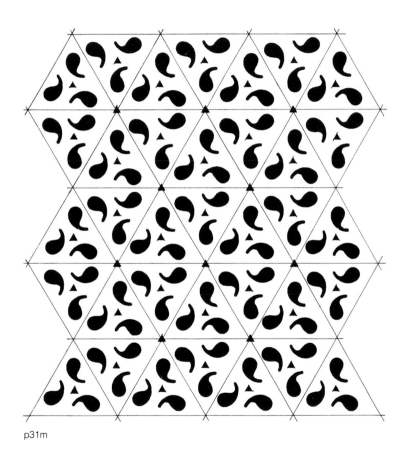

p31m

p4

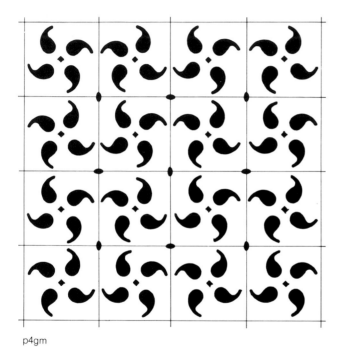

p4gm

p4mm

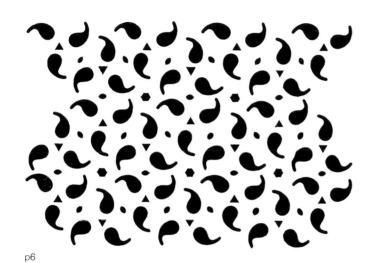

p6

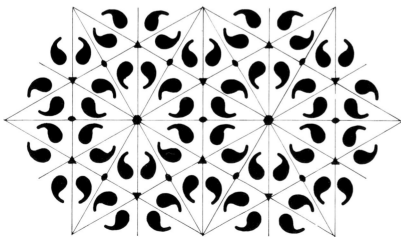

p6mm

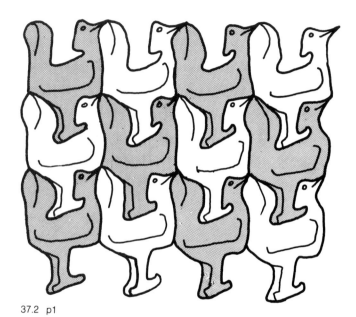

37.2 p1

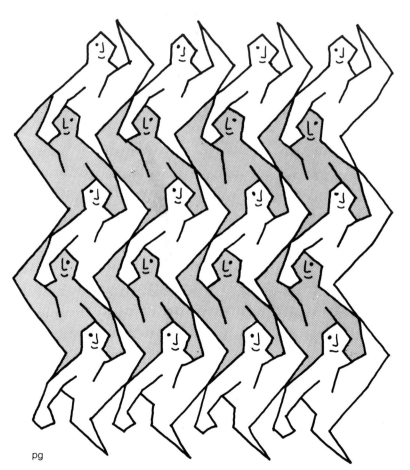

pg

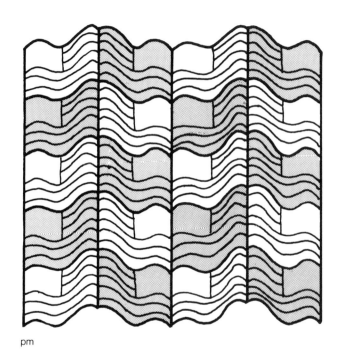

pm

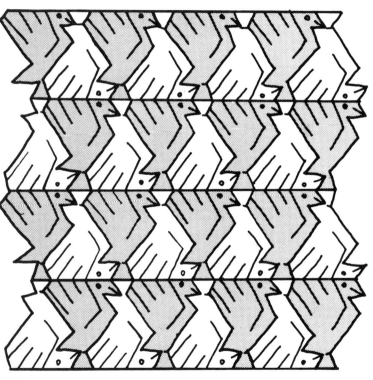

cm

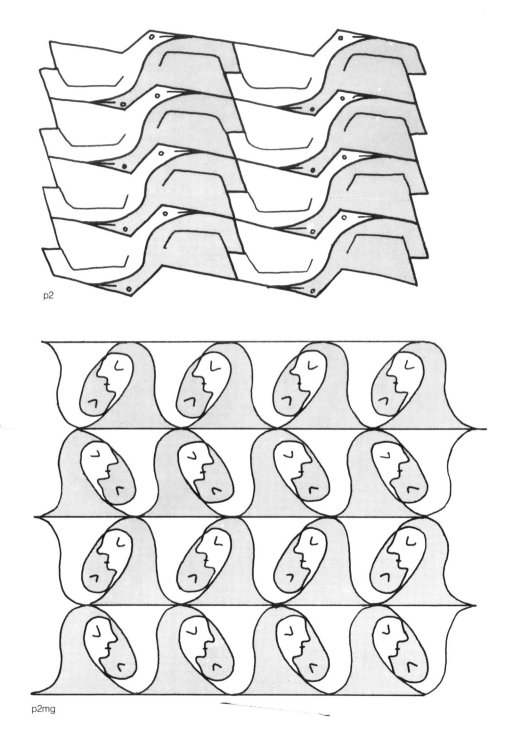

p2

p2mg

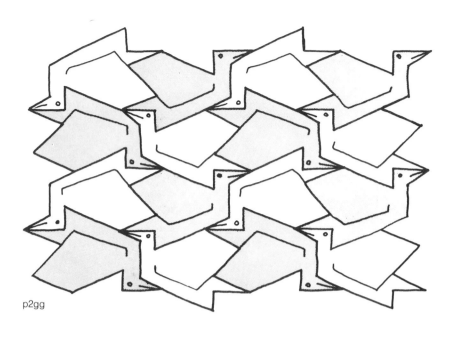

p2gg

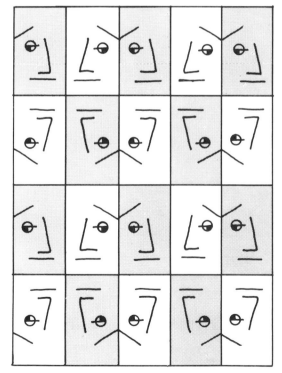

p2mm

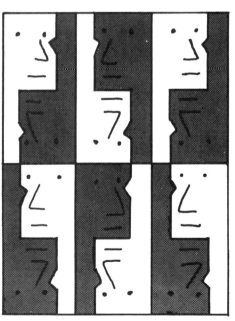

c2mm

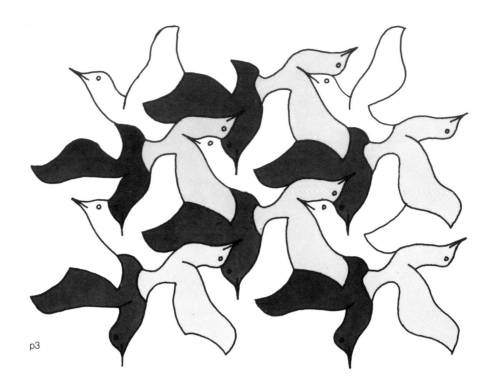

p3

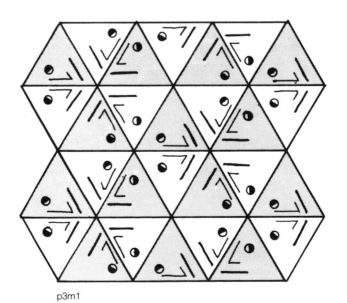

p3m1

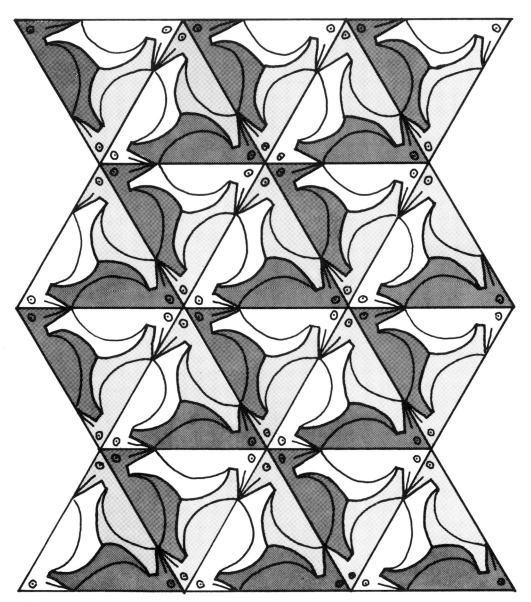

p31m

p4

p4gm

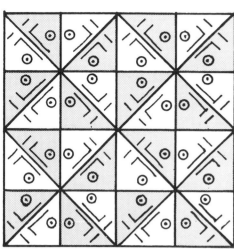

p4mm

p6

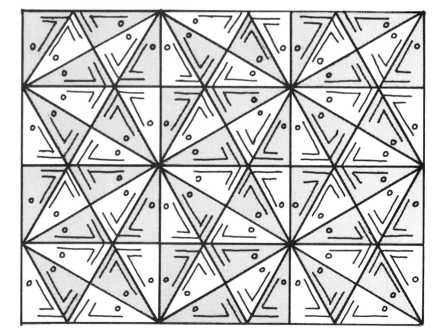

p6mm

37.3   1

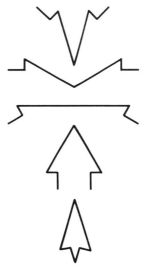

m

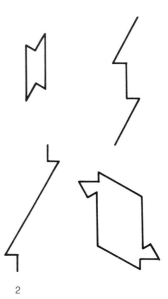

2

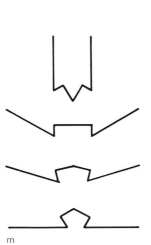

m

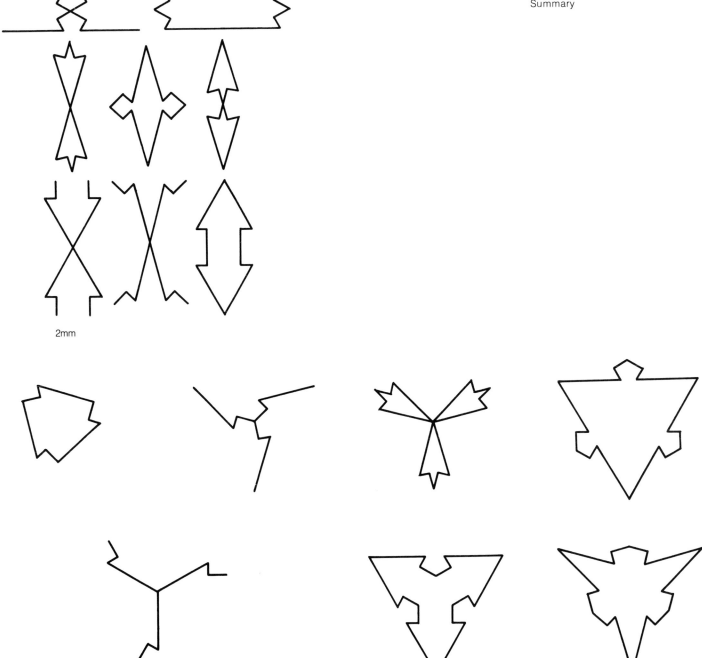

2mm

3

3m

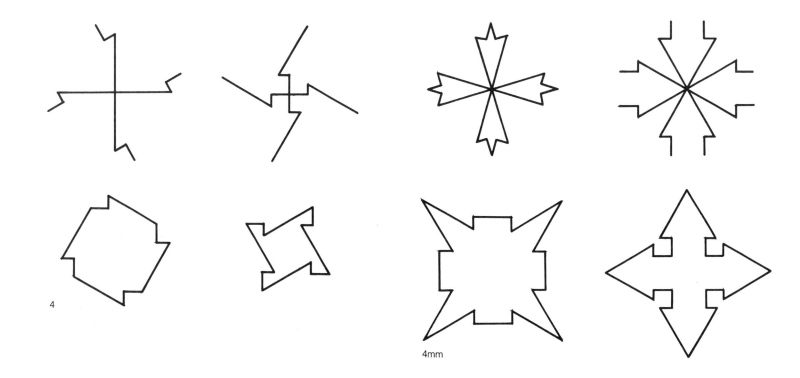

4

4mm

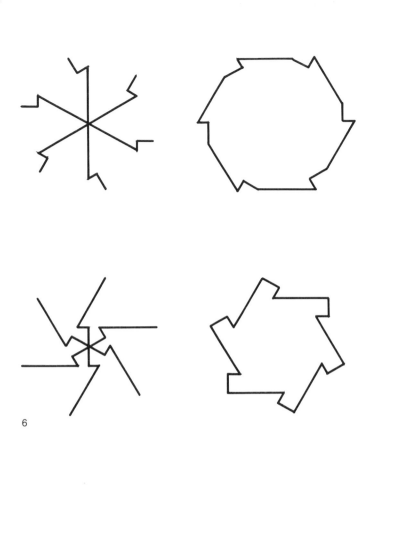

6

6mm

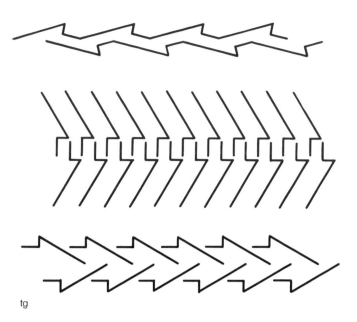

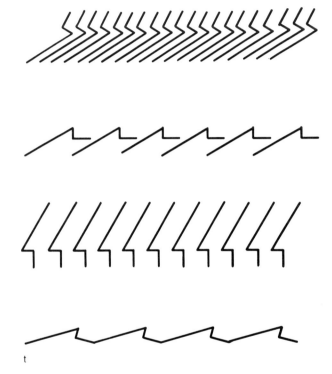

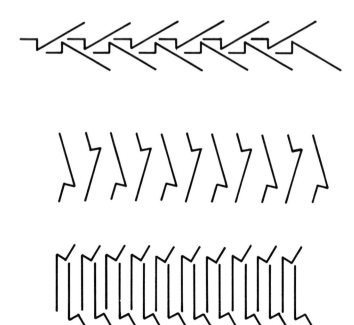

t

tg

tg

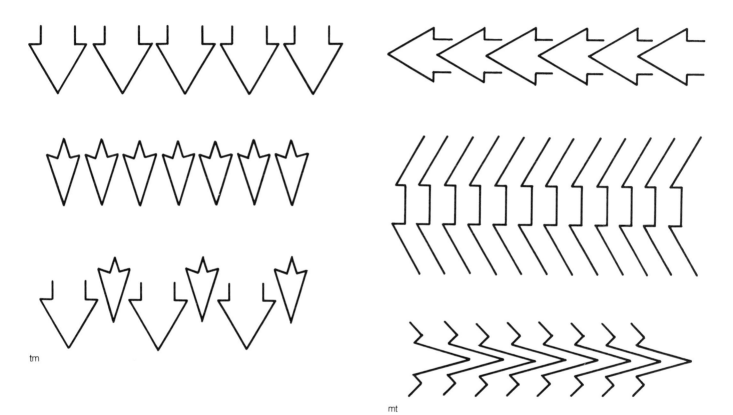

tm

mt

t2

t2

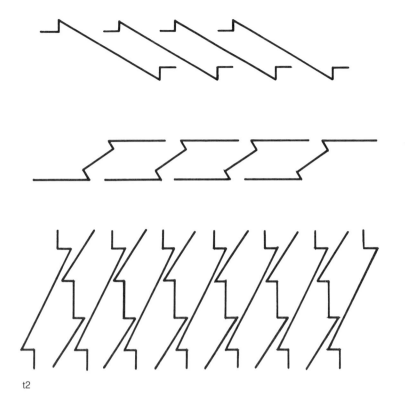

t2

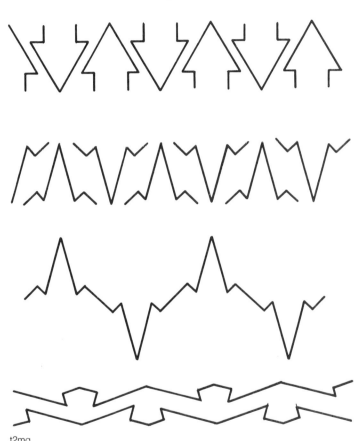

t2mg

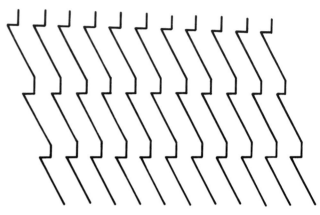

p1

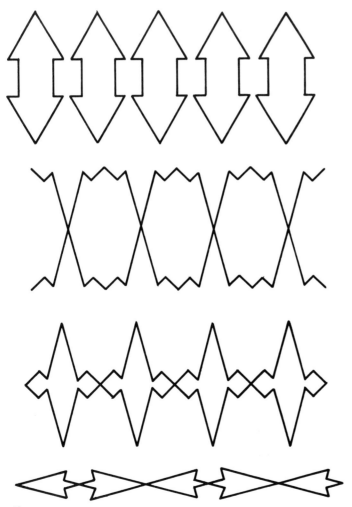

t2mm

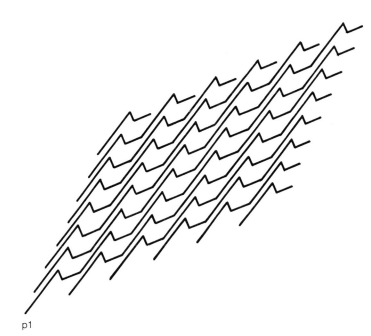

p1

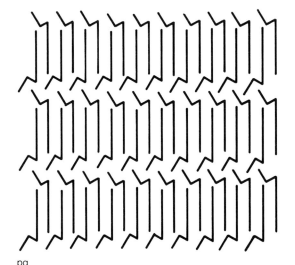

pg

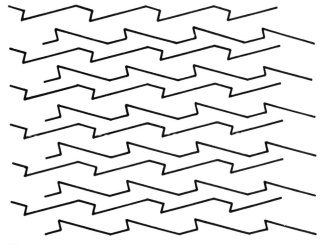

pg

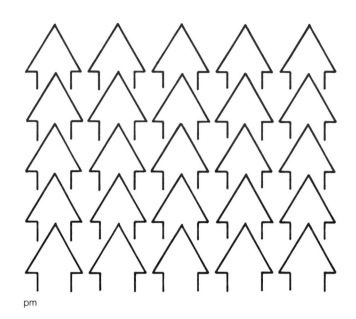

pm

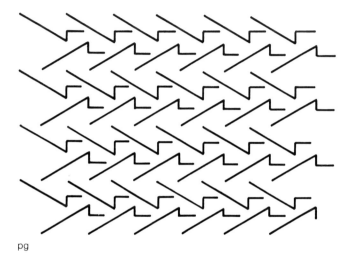

pg

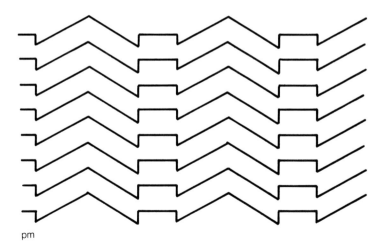

pm

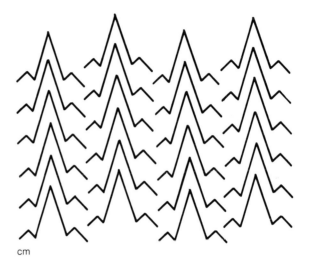

cm

pm

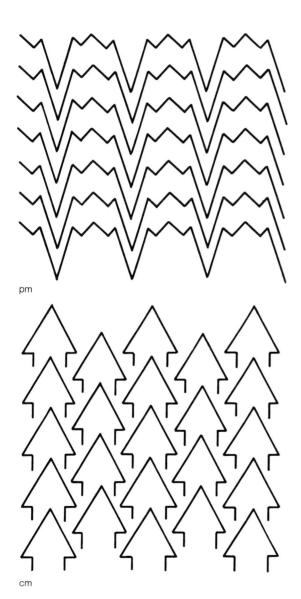

cm

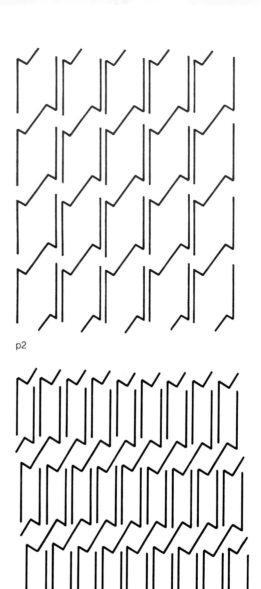

p2

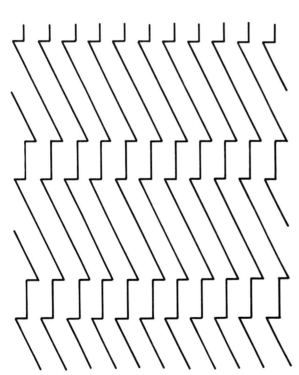

p2

p2

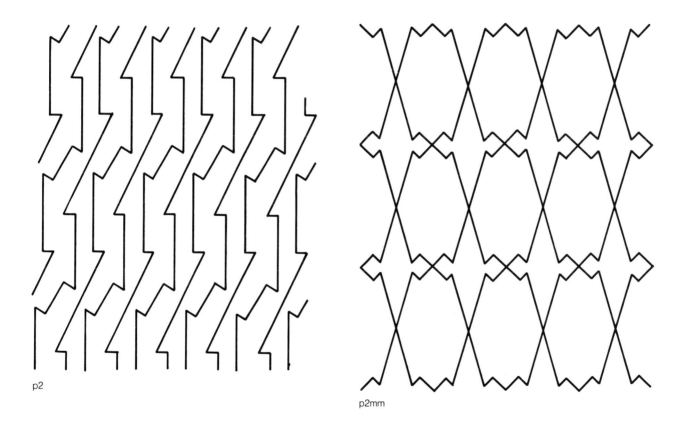

p2

p2mm

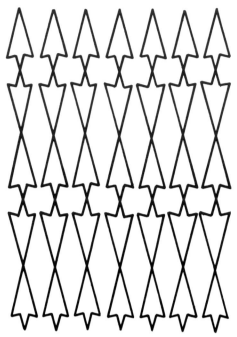

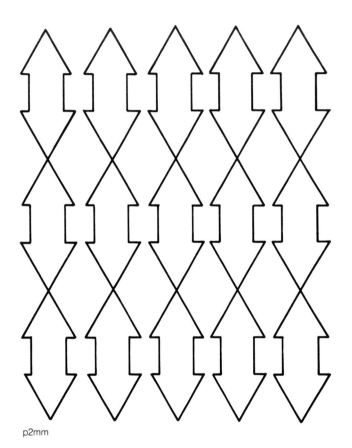

p2mm

p2mm

p2mg

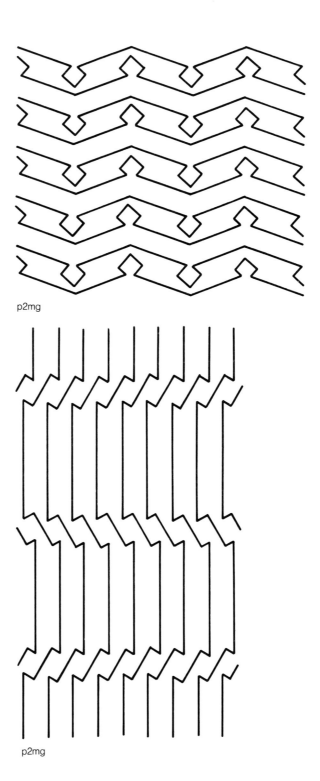

p2mg

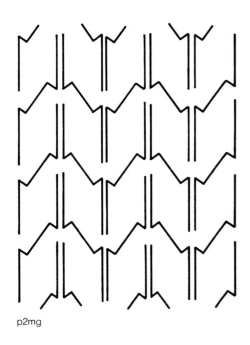

p2mg

p2mg

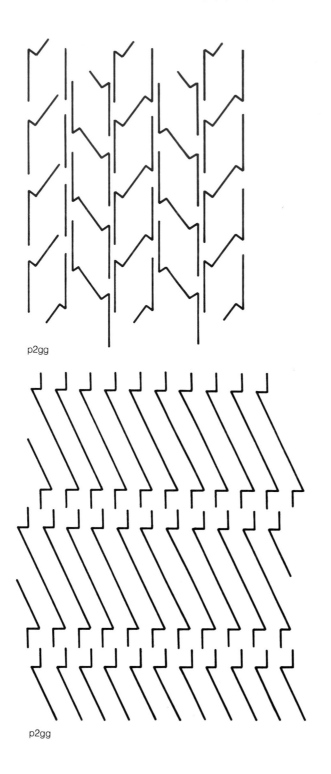

p2gg

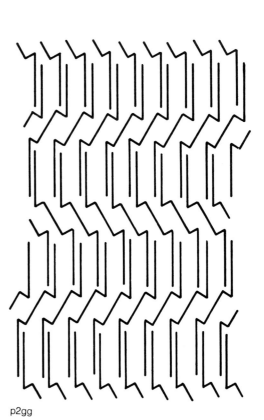

p2gg

p2gg

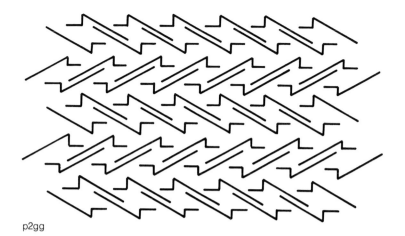

p2gg

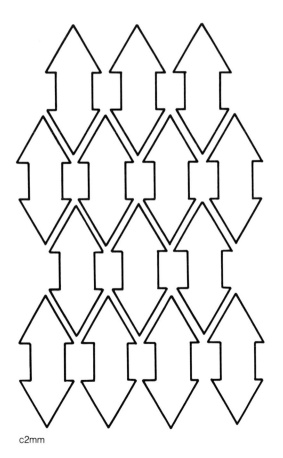

c2mm

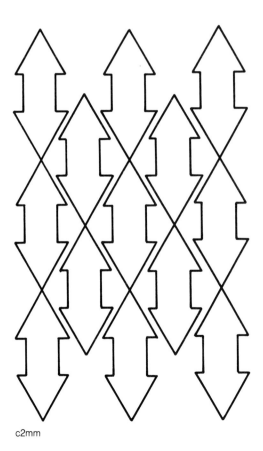

c2mm

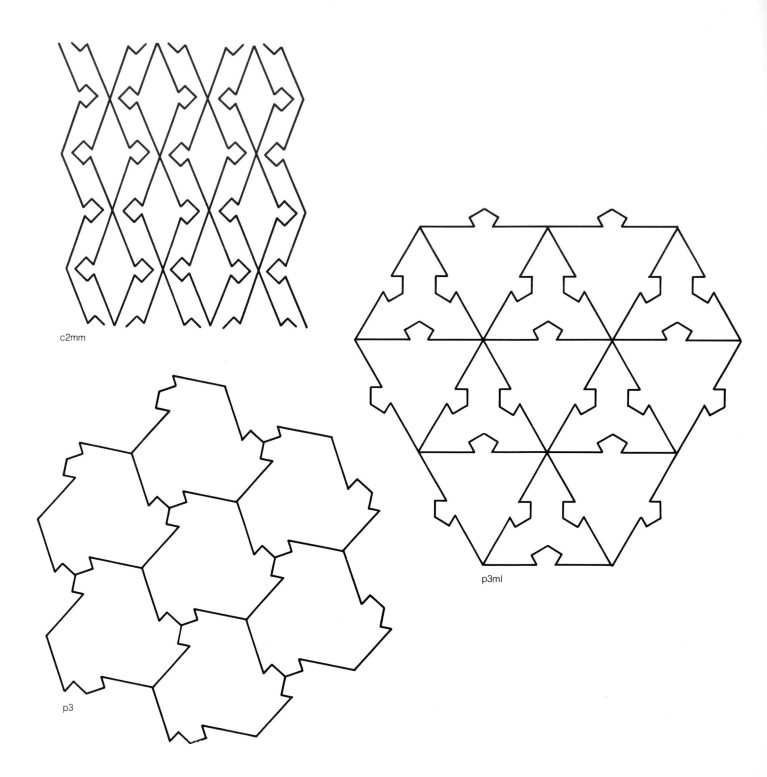

c2mm

p3

p3ml

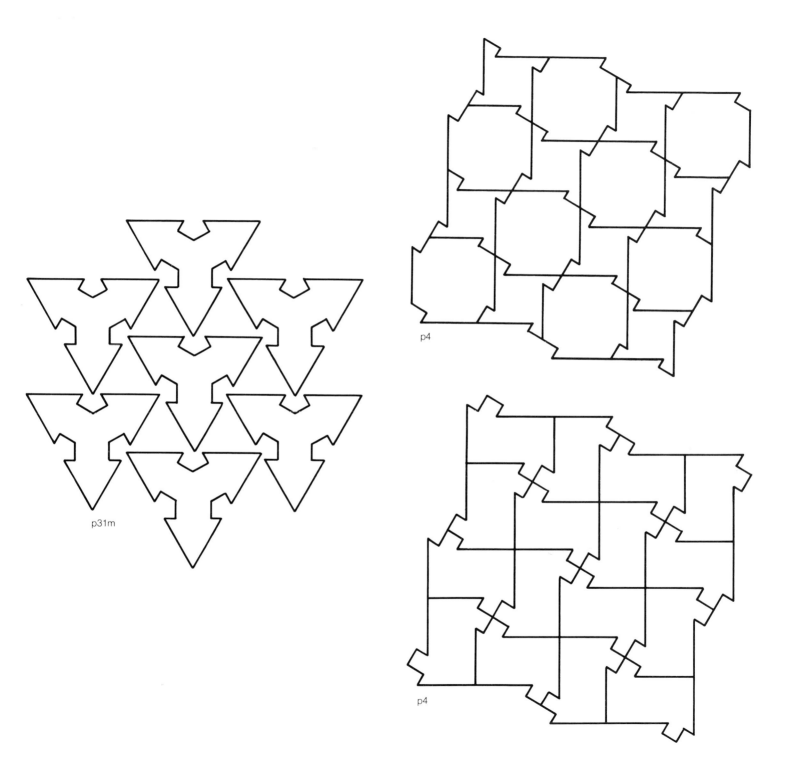

p31m

p4

p4

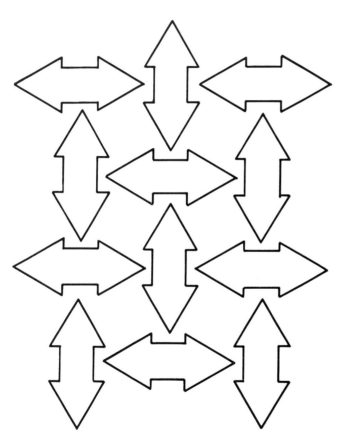

p4gm

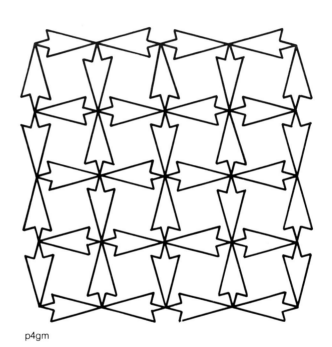

p4gm

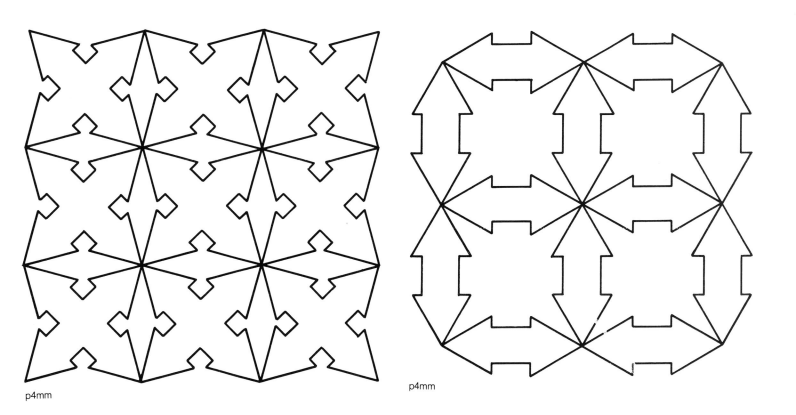

p4mm

p4mm

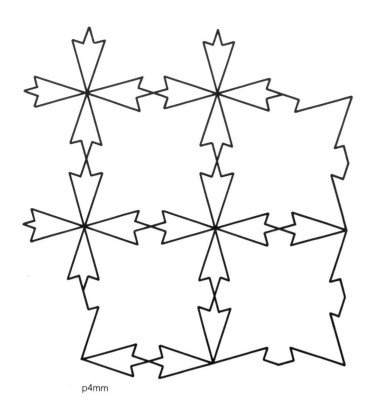

p4mm

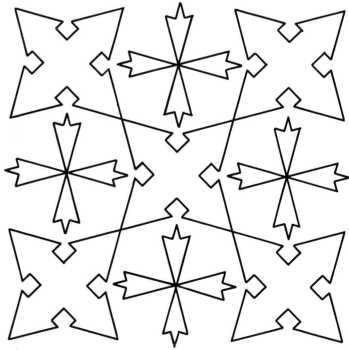

p4mm

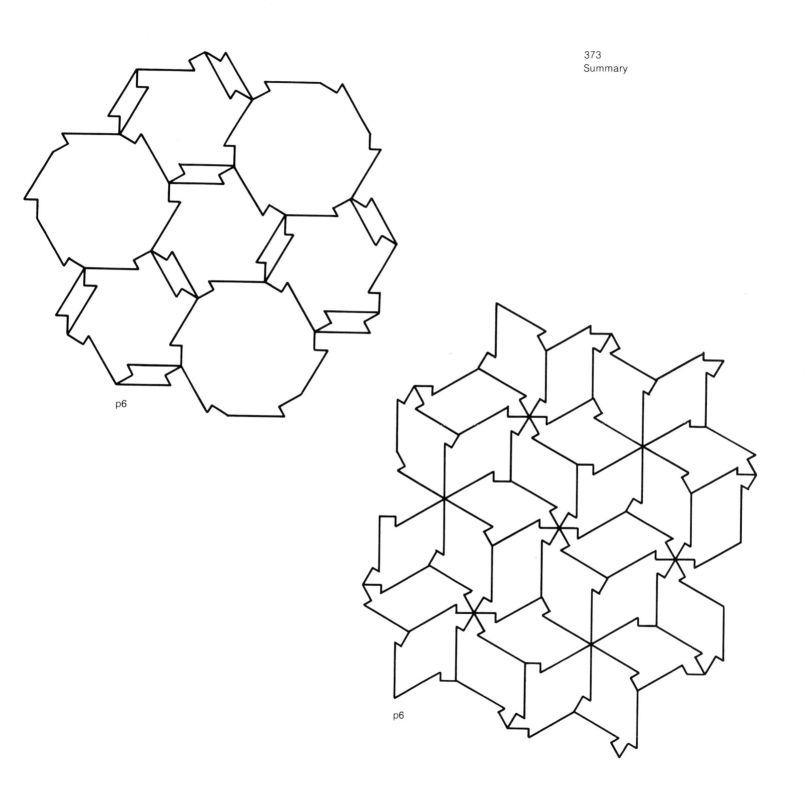

p6

p6

p6mm

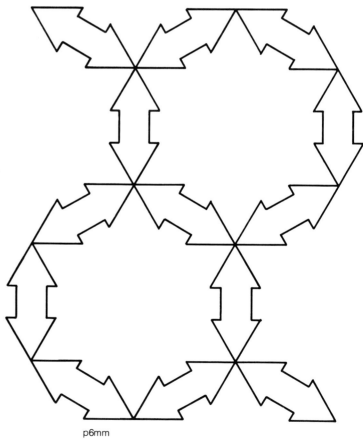

p6mm

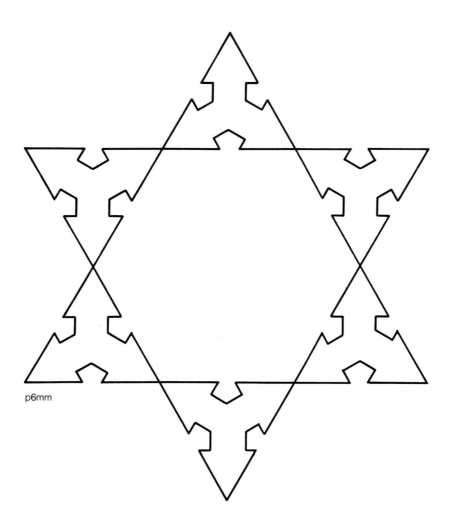

p6mm

Appendix
Derivations and the
Absence of Group *p*5

Recalcitrant Pentagons

Space and nature have decreed the absence of fivefold symmetry in patterns that cover a plane. No designer, however clever, can put aside this decree. You can see the effect of this stricture when you attempt to pack regular pentagons to obtain a lattice of points with pentagonal symmetry. You simply cannot do it. And neither could the German artist Albrecht Dürer. In figure **A.1**, redrawn from Dürer's work, see if you can identify the group designation of each arrangement. You might do the same for the design in figure **A.2** taken from a drawing by Johannes Kepler, the famous German astronomer, physicist, and mathematician. Again, try your luck with figure **A.3** which shows pentagons and pentagonal stars in two modern designs by Altair.

Notice in all these examples that the pentagons and stars, which themselves have fivefold symmetry, do not establish pentagonal symmetry within the overall pattern.

The Moors, who were the undisputed masters of repetitive design, produced in Cairo in the fourteenth century the pattern in figure **A.4**, which we first observed in figure 18.10. It was created for the leaf of a wooden door inlaid with ivory panels. You can easily find regular five- and ten-pointed stars, but do their five- and tenfold symmetries hold up under additional repetitions of the design? The design in figure **A.5**, which we have seen in figure 28.11, supplies the answer. The apparent pentagons on the sides of the original design are false. In reality they have only twofold symmetry so that the design, when extended, belongs to group *c2mm*.

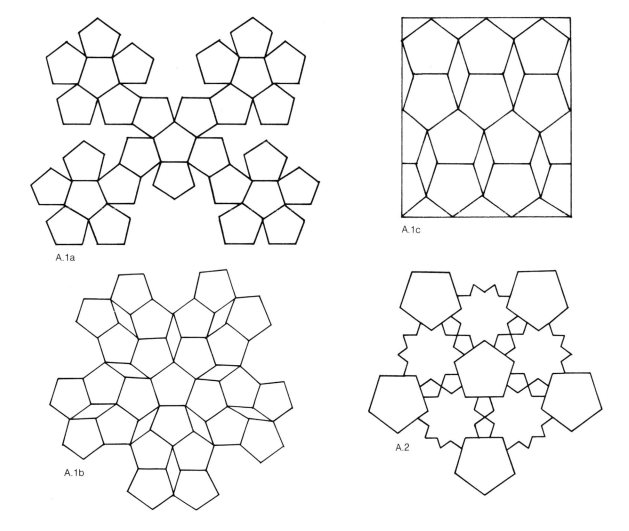

A.1a

A.1c

A.1b

A.2

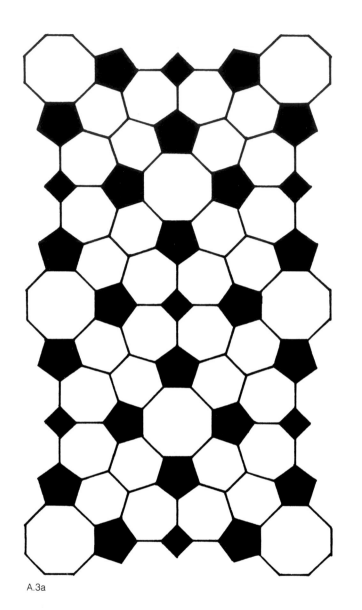

A.3a

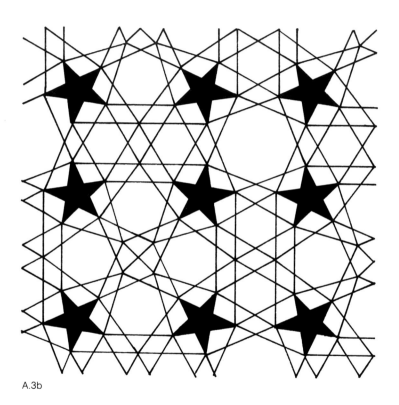

A.3b

A.4

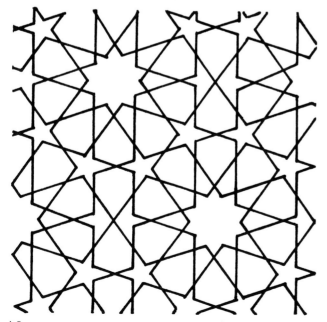

A.5

The Structure of Space

So why have Dürer, Kepler, the Moors, and all other designers throughout history found it impossible to create repetitive fivefold symmetries? Why has nature denied herself the pleasure of repetitive pentagonal arrangements?

The answer lies with the structure of space, an elucidation of which can be obtained through mathematics.

The General Case

Let us consider mathematically the general case: a rotocenter with n-fold symmetry at some point P in the plane. The only constraint we will put on n is that it be an integral number. Through how many degrees does the n-fold center rotate a design before the design repeats? The answer is 360°/n. With a fourfold rotocenter, for example, the design repeats every 360°/4 or 90°.

Assuming that this n-fold center is embedded in a repetitive design, let us mark in the plane the location of another rotocenter of exactly the same type, and let us assume that the second rotocenter lies closer than any other of the same type to the original rotocenter. The situation is diagramed in figure **A.6**a which shows two rotocenters of the same type, one at point P and one at point Q, as close together as possible.

Frame (b) of the figure shows the next step, when the rotocenter at Q acts on point P to shift it through the angle 360°/n into point P'. Continuing the process, we can activate the rotocenter at P' to shift point Q through the angle 360°/n to point Q'. Frame (c) shows the result: we obtain four different locations for the same rotocenter.

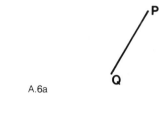

A.6a

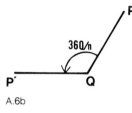

A.6b

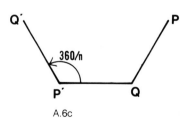

A.6c

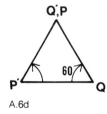

A.6d

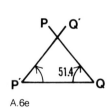

A.6e

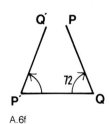

A.6f

All that remains is to look at the implications of this exercise when n takes different values. We can guess, for example, that points Q′ and P might coincide as in frame (d). In that case, the rotocenters will lie at the vertexes of an equilateral triangle where angle 360°/n equals 60° and n = 6. This instance reveals that sixfold rotocenters can exist in a plane at 60° to one another.

What about rotocenters of higher order than six? Frame (e) shows the situation that arises with sevenfold centers. When n = 7, 360°/n = 51.4°, an angle which is so sharp or acute that the line between the rotocenters at P and Q crosses the line between the rotocenters at P′ and Q′. The result is that the original point P lies closer to P′ than it does to Q—a result that violates our original assumption that no rotocenter of the same type lies closer to P than Q. We could, of course, take P′ as the point closest to P and go through the exercise again, but we would get the same result: a new location for the rotocenter would fall even closer to the original rotocenter than the closest one! Since rotocenters of still higher order produce still more acute angles, we conclude that repetitive rotocenters of higher order than six cannot exist in a plane.

What about fivefold centers? Frame (f) shows why they cannot exist. The angle 360°/n or 72° swings the rotocenters so that point Q′ lies closer to P than Q. Thus with fivefold centers as with centers of higher order than six, we run into the same contradiction. We find rotocenters separated by less than a minimum separation.

Frame (g) shows the situation for fourfold centers. There the angle 360°/n equals 90° so that lines PQ and QP′ stick straight out from P′Q at right angles. The rotocenters mark the vertexes of a square. The separation between P and Q′ exactly equals the minimum separation between P and Q. We conclude, therefore, that centers of fourfold rotation can coexist in a plane.

Frame (h) verifies the existence of threefold centers. The centers at P′ and Q rotate lines QP and P′Q′ through 120° so that points P and Q′ are separated by exactly twice the distance between P and Q.

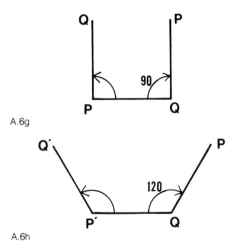

A.6g

A.6h

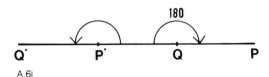

A.6i

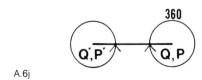

A.6j

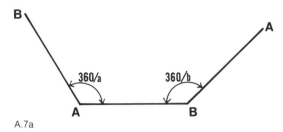

A.7a

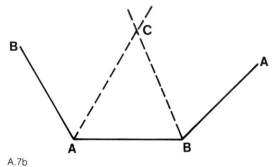

A.7b

The example of coexisting twofold centers illustrated in frame (i) shows that when $n = 2$, $360°/n = 180°$, so that the angle of 180° rotates lines Q'P' and QP into direct alignment with line P'Q. Consequently, coexisting twofold centers are linearly aligned.

Frame (j) documents the case when $n = 1$. Since the angle of rotation equals 360°, the rotocenter at Q returns the rotocenter at P' to P and the rotocenter at P moves Q' back to Q. Consequently we conclude that singlefold rotocenters can also coexist in the plane. What this whole exercise reveals is that only one-, two-, three-, four-, and sixfold rotocenters have a role in repetitive arrays. A little mathematics has gone a long way. Instead of drawing countless patterns to explore whether repetitive fivefold centers can exist, we reviewed in a few moments the general case to conclude, as did

Barlow in 1897 when he developed the proof [1: pp. 527–620], that for all people and for all time only one-, two-, three-, four-, and sixfold centers form repetitive two-dimensional patterns. When you consider the number of man-years the Moors and others must have expended in trial-and-error searching for regular pentagonal arrangements, you cannot help but marvel at the beauty and economy of Barlow's proof.

How Rotocenters Combine
More mathematics of the same sort can take us even further. We can determine which rotocenters will combine with which other rotocenters. This determination was first made rigorously by P. LeCorbeiller and A. L. Loeb in 1967 [14].

Taking again the general case, suppose you have two different types of rotocenters, one type located at each of the two points marked A and the other type located at the two points marked B in figure **A.7**a. Let us assume that the rotocenters at points A shift points B through $360°/a$ and the rotocenters at points B shift

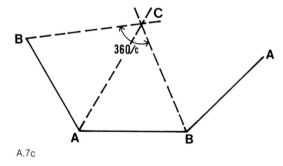

A.7c

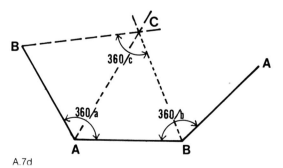

A.7d

points A through $360°/b$. Now suppose that still a third type of rotocenter exists. Where will it be located? The answer is straightforward. As shown in frame (b) it must be located at a point equidistant from both the points marked A. Only if it is equidistant from these points can it shift one into the other. Consequently it must fall on the dotted line that bisects angle ABA. Similarly, that third rotocenter must also lie equidistant from the two points marked B, that is to say, it must lie on the dotted line that bisects angle BAB. The exact position of the new rotocenter is therefore fixed: at point C marked by the intersection of the two angle bisectors. We will designate the rotational angle of this rotocenter at C as $360°/c$. Frame (c) shows how it sweeps one point B into the other through an angle of $360°/c$. Notice also that the dotted line AC bisects the angle $360°/c$ since point A lies at equal distances from both points B.

In conclusion then, let us consider the angles of the triangle ABC in frame (d). We know that they must total to $180°$—the angle sum of any triangle. Making use of the angle bisectors we can add the three angles of the triangle in this way:

$$1/2(360°/a) + 1/2(360°/b) + 1/2(360°/c) = 180°$$

where $1/2(360°/a)$ equals one-half of the rotational angle at point A, $1/2(360°/b)$ equals one-half the rotational angle at point B, etc. Simplification leads to the expression

$$180°/a + 180°/b + 180°/c = 180°$$

or, more simply still,

$$\frac{1}{a} + \frac{1}{b} + \frac{1}{c} = 1$$

This result is a marvel of economy. Remembering that $a, b,$ and c can only have values of 6, 4, 3, 2, and 1, the formula says that when taken three at a time the fractions 1/6, 1/4, 1/3, 1/2, and 1/1 must sum to unity. How many combinations can you write? Just these three:

$$\frac{1}{6} + \frac{1}{3} + \frac{1}{2} = 1$$

$$\frac{1}{4} + \frac{1}{4} + \frac{1}{2} = 1$$

$$\frac{1}{3} + \frac{1}{3} + \frac{1}{3} = 1$$

You can shuffle the order of the fractions within each combination and write, for example,

$$\frac{1}{3} + \frac{1}{2} + \frac{1}{6} = 1$$

instead of

$$\frac{1}{6} + \frac{1}{3} + \frac{1}{2} = 1$$

but that change is not significant. You are limited to the three basic combinations.

Pie Charts

These permissible combinations can be described geometrically by means of pie charts. Figure **A.8**a shows how the sixth part of a circle—a sector of $60°$—combines with half a circle and a third part—sectors of $180°$ and $120°$—to make a whole pie. Frame (b) illustrates how two quarters plus a half—$90°$. $90°$, and $180°$—make a whole. Frame (c) pictures the sum of three $120°$ sectors. No other combinations of three fractional parts are possible. A quarter part and a third part of a circle cannot combine, for example, for the sector which remained would equal 5/12, and 5/12 is not one of Barlow's permissible fractions.

Again you can appreciate the economy of the mathematical derivation. Without drawing a line you know incontrovertibly that the presence of sixfold centers dictates the presence of threefold and twofold centers. You know that one type of fourfold center ensures the presence of another type of fourfold center as well as interacting twofold centers. You know that patterns with three types of threefold centers are possible, but that fourfold centers cannot combine with sixfold or with threefold centers.

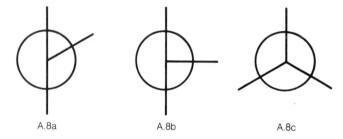

A.8a   A.8b   A.8c

Excluded Combinations

Let's explore this last impossibility. What really happens when you attempt to combine threefold with fourfold centers? Figure **A.9** tells the story. Point A marks the location of a threefold center and point B the location of a fourfold center that rotates point A through 90° to establish point C. Point C then represents a threefold center that rotates point B through 120° to mark the location of a fourfold center at point D. When you continue in this manner to alternate three- and fourfold centers you find, as illustrated in frame (a), that the line EF crosses the end of line AB, that the circuit does not end at point A where it began. In fact, as you continue to alternate three- and fourfold centers you must make five full circuits before you arrive again at the starting point. Frame (b) shows the figure that results after five circuits. It contains twelve threefold centers like points A, C, and E, and twelve fourfold centers like points B, D, and F. The meaning of the 5/12 which arises in the formula

$$\frac{1}{3} + \frac{1}{4} + \frac{5}{12} = 1$$

is clear. It indicates that twelve threefold and twelve fourfold centers make a closed star after five circuits.

In a different vein, M. C. Escher produced two works of art that can be interpreted as attempts to cover a plane with three- and fourfold rotocenters. They are shown in figures **A.10** and **A.11**. See if you can find the two types of centers in each picture. Are there any true threefold or fourfold centers?

The Third Dimension

The pattern in figure A.11 looks as if it was drawn on the surface of a large sphere and you might wonder if you could arrange regular three- and fourfold centers on a surface that wrapped around on itself to make a closed three-dimensional form. The octahedron shown in figure **A.12** whose faces are eight regular triangles shows that the answer is yes. The centers of the triangles mark points of threefold rotation, and the joins of four lines, where four triangles meet, mark points of fourfold rotation. Those centers alternate continuously around the figure. It is interesting to observe that the three- and fourfold axes pass clear through the octahedron, so that each threefold axis penetrates two triangles on

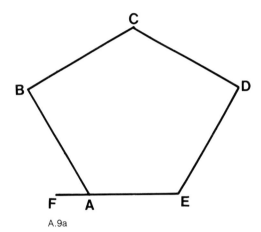

A.9a

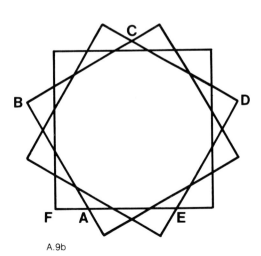

A.9b

opposite sides, and each fourfold axis passes through two opposing vertexes. From either end of each axis, therefore, the entire figure has three- or fourfold symmetry. Similarly, through the centers of each pair of opposite edges the figure has twofold symmetry.

Those axes may be hard to visualize if you are unfamiliar with an octahedron and cannot hold one in your hand. It happens that the more familiar cube illustrated in frame (b) contains the same types of axes. Threefold axes pass through opposite three-way corners, fourfold axes penetrate the centers of opposite square faces, and twofold axes rotate the figure about the midpoints of opposite edges.

What about the dodecahedron in frame (c)? Can you visualize its axes of fivefold, threefold, and twofold symmetry?

The point, of course, is not to describe exhaustively the symmetries of three-dimensional forms but to indicate that many elements of symmetry, such as axes of rotation, which occur in the two-dimensional plane occur also in three-dimensional space. But these elements combine differently. Whereas three- and fourfold axes do not combine in a plane they can join with one

another on the surface of a polyhedron. Whereas repetitive fivefold axes cannot occur in two dimensions, they can exist in three. There is more freedom in three dimensions than in two. Corresponding to the seventeen two-dimensional patterns, three-dimensional space permits 230 different patterns. But these 230 patterns are just as discrete and circumscribed as the seventeen. There do not exist 231 or 234 or some other number of three-dimensional groups—only 230—no more and no less—for all of time.

Four Twofold Centers
Before we leave the discussion of which types of rotocenters can combine in the plane, we must pick up a lost thread. Let us return to frame (i) of figure A.6. There we saw a line of twofold centers like a string of beads. We assumed that the beads had the minimum possible spacing. From our studies of group $t2$, however, we learned that one set of twofold centers gives rise to another set with the result that two different types of twofold centers alternate with one another along the same line.

A.10

A.11

A.12a

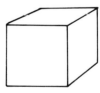

A.12b

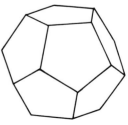

A.12c

Figure **A.13**a shows a line of alternating twofold centers. Recalling the exercise diagrammed in figure A.7, we can ask where the location of a possible third type of rotocenter might be. Obviously it must lie at the intersection of the bisectors of the 180° angles at the twofold centers. Because those bisectors meet at infinity, that third rotocenter must also lie at infinity. This result is mathematically consistent since

$$\frac{1}{2} + \frac{1}{2} + \frac{1}{\infty} = 1$$

But on this side of infinity we are left with a $t2$ linear band rather than a plane-filling group. How can we prove that twofold centers combine to make plane groups?

We must try a different approach. Let us add a rotocenter of some unspecified type next to the band. It is designated by the cross in frame (b). The operation of the twofold centers will shift the cross to the additional positions indicated in frame (c). Now we can ask what type of rotocenter the crosses represent. If they represent three-, four-, or sixfold centers, they will rotate the original line of twofold centers so that it crosses itself, the implication being that some of the twofold centers will then lie closer together than the original centers

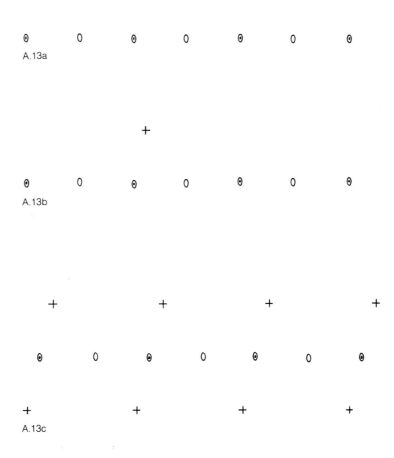

A.13a

A.13b

A.13c

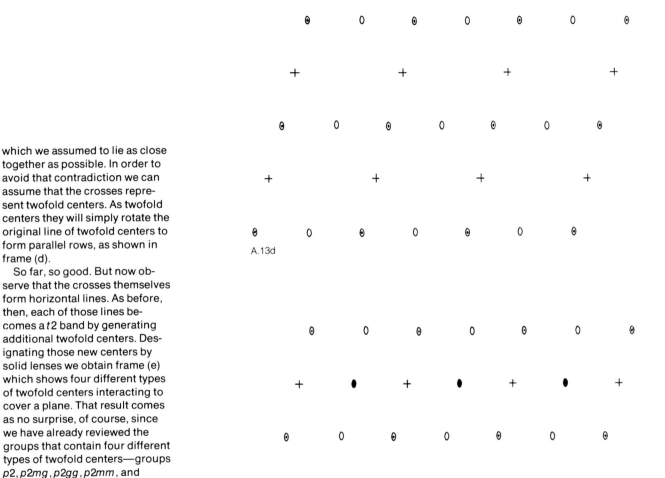

A.13d

A.13e

which we assumed to lie as close together as possible. In order to avoid that contradiction we can assume that the crosses represent twofold centers. As twofold centers they will simply rotate the original line of twofold centers to form parallel rows, as shown in frame (d).

So far, so good. But now observe that the crosses themselves form horizontal lines. As before, then, each of those lines becomes a $t2$ band by generating additional twofold centers. Designating those new centers by solid lenses we obtain frame (e) which shows four different types of twofold centers interacting to cover a plane. That result comes as no surprise, of course, since we have already reviewed the groups that contain four different types of twofold centers—groups $p2$, $p2mg$, $p2gg$, $p2mm$, and $c2mm$.

Limited Combinations
At this point we have reviewed all permissible combinations of rotocenters: 2222, 333, 442, and 632. We have seen how these combinations arise and proved that in covering a plane no other combinations are possible.

Exercises

1. Assuming wherever possible that the pattern is infinitely extended, give group designations for the following figures:

(a) A.1a
(b) A.1b
(c) A.1c
(d) A.2
(e) A.3a
(f) A.3b
(g) A.10
(h) A.11

2. What is the group designation of figure A.14—a design by M. C. Escher? Do the flowers have $5m$ symmetry?

A.14

Bibliography

Historical References

1. Barlow, W. *Scientific Proceedings of the Royal Dublin Society*, VIII, Part VI. Dec. 20, 1897, pp. 527–620

2. Dürer, Albrecht. *Vier Bücher von Menschlicber Proportion*. Nuremberg, 1528

3. Fedorov, E. S. *Zapiski Mineralogicheskogo Imperatorskogo S. Peterburgskogo Obshchestva* (2), 28. 1891, pp. 345–390

4. Fricke, R., and Klein, F. *Vorlesungen über die Theorie der automorphen Funktionen*. Vol. 1. Leipzig: Teubner, 1897

5. Kepleri, Joannis. *Astronomi Opera Omnia*. Vol. 5. 1864, pp. 115–116

6. Pólya, G., and Niggli, P. *Zeitschrift für Kristallographie und Minerologie*, 60, 1964, pp. 278–298

7. Speiser, A. *Theorie der Gruppen von endlicher Ordnung*. 4th ed. Basel: Birkhäuser, 1956

8. Steiger, von Franz. *Commentarii Mathematici Helvetici*, 8, 1936, pp. 235–249

Symmetry and Mathematics

9. Bernal, I.; Hamilton, W. C.; and Ricci, J. S. *Symmetry*. San Francisco: W. H. Freeman and Company, 1972

10. Birkhoff, George D. *Aesthetic Measure*. Cambridge: Harvard University Press, 1933

11. Coxeter, H. M. S. *Introduction to Geometry*. New York: John Wiley & Sons, Inc., 1961

12. Grossman I., and Magnus, W. *Groups and Their Graphs*. New York: Random House, 1964

13. Hilbert D., and Cohn-Vossen, S. *Geometry and the Imagination*. New York: Chelsea Publishing Company, 1956

14. Loeb, Arthur L. *Color and Symmetry*. New York: John Wiley & Sons, Inc., 1971

15. Senechal, Marjorie, and Fleck, George, eds. *Patterns of Symmetry*. Amherst: University of Massachusetts Press, 1977

16. Shubnikov, A. V., and Koptsik, V. A. *Symmetry in Science and Art*. New York: Plenum Press, 1974

17. Steinhaus, H. *Mathematical Snapshots*. New York: Oxford University Press, 1969

18. Tóth, L. Fejes. *Regular Figures*. New York: The Macmillan Company, 1964

19. Weyl, Hermann. *Symmetry*. Princeton: Princeton University Press, 1952

Crystallography

20. Buerger, Martin J. *Elementary*

Crystallography. New York: John Wiley and Sons, Inc., 1963

21. Henry N. F. M., and Lonsdale, K. *International Tables for X-Ray Crystallography: Vol. 1 Symmetry Groups*. Birmingham: Kynock Press, 1952

22. Wells, A. F. *The Third Dimension in Chemistry*. Oxford: At the Clarendon Press, 1956

23. Wood, Elizabeth A. *Crystals and Light*. New York: D. Van Nostrand Company, Inc., 1964

Source Books on Design

24. Albarn, K.; Smith, J. M.; Steele, S.; and Walker, D. *The Language of Pattern*. New York: Harper and Row, 1974

25. Appleton, Leroy H. *American Indian Design and Decoration*. New York: Dover Publications, Inc., 1971

26. Audsley, W. and G. *Designs and Patterns from Historic Ornaments*. New York: Dover Publications, Inc., 1968

27. Bourgoin, J. *Theorie de l'Ornement*. Paris, 1883

28. Bourgoin, J. *Arabic Geometrical Pattern and Design*. New York: Dover Publications, Inc., 1973

29. Christie, Archibald H. *Pattern Design*. New York: Dover Publications. Inc., 1969

30. Douglas F. H., and Harnoncourt, R. D. *Indian Art of the United States*. New York: Museum of Modern Art, 1941

31. Dreyfus, Henry. *Symbol Sourcebook*. New York: McGraw-Hill Book Company, 1972

32. Durant, Stuart. *Victorian Ornamental Design*. New York: St. Martin's Press, Inc., 1972

33. Dye, Daniel Sheets. *A Grammar of Chinese Ornament*. Cambridge: Harvard University Press, 1937

34. Enciso, Jorge. *Design Motifs of Ancient Mexico*. New York: Dover Publications, Inc., 1953

35. Gillon, Jr., Edmund V. *Geometric Design and Ornament*. New York: Dover Publications, Inc.,1969

36. Gillon, Jr., Edmund V. *Victorian Stencils for Design and Decoration*. New York: Dover Publications, Inc., 1968

37. Holiday, Ensor. *Altair Designs*. New York: Pantheon Books, various dates (Vol. 4, 1978)

38. Hornung, Clarence P. *Hornung's Handbook of Designs and Devices*. New York: Dover Publications, Inc., 1946

39. Hornung, Clarence P. *Allover Patterns*. New York: Dover Publications, Inc., 1975

40. Humbert, Claude. *Ornamental Design*. New York: The Viking Press, 1970

41. Jones, Owen. *The Grammar of Ornament*. New York: Van Nostrand Reinhold Company, 1972

42. Koch, Rudolf. *The Book of Signs*. New York: Dover Publications, Inc., 1955

43. Lehner, Ernst. *Symbols, Signs & Signets*. New York: Dover Publications. Inc., 1969

44. Meyer, Franz Sales. *Handbook of Ornament*. New York: Dover Publications, Inc., 1957

45. Mizoguchi, Saburo. *Arts of Japan 1: Design Motifs*. New York: Weatherhill, 1973

46. Mold, Josephine. *Tessellations*. Cambridge: At the University Press, 1969

47. Sides, Dorothy Smith. *Decorative Arts of the Southwestern Indians*. New York: Dover Publications, Inc., 1961

48. Speltz, Alexander. *The Styles of Ornament*. New York: Dover Publications, Inc., 1959

49. Tuer, Andrew W. *Japanese Stencil Designs*. New York: Dover Publications, Inc. 1967

M. C. Escher

50. Ernst, Bruno. *The Magic Mirror of M. C. Escher*. New York: Random House, 1976

51. Escher, M. C. *The Graphic Work of M. C. Escher*. New York: Meredith Press, 1967

52. Locher, J. L., ed. *The World of M. C. Escher*. New York: Harry N. Abrams, 1971

53. Macgillavry, Caroline H. *Fantasy & Symmetry*. New York: Harry N. Abrams, 1976

Special References

54. Hawley, Walter A. *Oriental Rugs*. New York: Dover Publications, Inc., 1970

55. Heesch, H., and Kiensle, O. *Flächenschlub*. Berlin: Springer-Verlag, 1963

56. James, George Wharton. *Indian Blankets*. New York: Dover Publications, Inc., 1974

57. March L., and Steadman, P. *The Geometry of Environment*. Cambridge: The MIT Press, 1971

58. Payne-Gaposchkin, Cecilia. *Introduction to Astronomy*. New York: Prentice Hall, 1954

59. Safford C. L., and Bishop, R. *America's Quilts and Coverlets*. New York: Weathervane Books, 1974

60. Stravinsky, Igor *Poetics of Music*. New York: Random House, 1960

61. Taylor, Brian Bruce. *Le Corbusier et Pessac 1914–1928*. Paris: Spadem, 1972

Index

The numbers before the colon are group designations; those with a decimal are figures; the others indicate pages.